SOLVING BEHAVIOR PROBLEMS IN AUTISM

*Improving Communication with
Visual Strategies*

Linda A. Hodgdon, M.ED., CCC-SLP

QUIRKROBERTS
PUBLISHING

© 1999
Fifth Printing 2005
QuirkRoberts Publishing
P.O. Box 71
Troy, Michigan 48099-0071
Telephone: (248) 879-2598
Fax: (248) 879-2599

Original Illustrations: Rachel Hopkins.
Book Design: Frank G. Slanczka.

Picture Communication Symbols (pages 141, 142, 152, 162, 169, 174, 175, 178, 179, 180, 191, 192, 193, 205) used with permission: Mayer-Johnson Co., P.O. Box 1579, Solana Beach, CA 92075.
The Family Circus reprinted with special permission of King Features Syndicate.
Kroger logo used with permission: Kroger, Cincinnati, OH.
Betty Crocker and General Mills are registered trademarks used with permission: General Mills, Minneapolis, MN.
Old El Paso, Progresso and Pillsbury are registered trademarks used with permission: Pillsbury, Minneapolis, MN.
SuperKmart logo used with permission: Kmart Corporation, Troy, MI.

ISBN-10: 0-9616786-2-3
ISBN-13: 978-0-9616786-2-3

Library of Congress Catalog Card Number: 99-093451

Great care has been taken to protect the privacy of students and their families. The names of real students have been changed. Case histories and incidents described are compilations of numerous teacher-parent-student situations. Any relationship to real people is purely unintentional.

Dedicated to Carrie and Jordan and Caleb and "Q"
who taught me a lot about behavior.

*...turning your ear to wisdom and
applying your heart to understanding...*

Proverbs 2:2

...making wise the simple...

Psalm 19:7

Table of Contents

VI

X

Introduction

When *Visual Strategies for Improving Communication* was written it was received enthusiastically by both professionals and parents. That book was able to clearly describe and clarify a communication approach that has been gaining recognition because of its effectiveness when communicating with students who experience autism and other moderate to severe communication disorders. The approach is simple. Recognizing that students have different learning styles leads to the discovery that many of these students are *visual* learners. That means they understand what they *see* better than they understand what they *hear.* The significance of this observation has immeasurable implications considering how much social interaction and educational instruction depend on auditory-verbal communication. *Visual Strategies for Improving Communication* presents a framework for understanding how these students comprehend; how they communicate. It then provides a wealth of strategies, emphasizing the use of visual tools, for supporting their communication interactions and educational instruction.

Although the original outline for *Visual Strategies for Improving Communication* contained a chapter targeted at solving behavior problems, it became immediately apparent that talking about behavior required a greater depth of discussion than would fit into the format of that book. This author did not want to create an illusion that visual tools would become a "quick fix", like the Band-Aid that "cures" the wound. Granted, there are those times when visual tools do provide that "magical touch" to solve a problem or prevent a disaster. Many times, visual tools provide the support that is needed to avoid problems and facilitate the successful participation of students.

There is a danger in continually implementing behavior management strategies that skim the surface without understanding the bigger picture... the *causes* of difficulties. The result of surface intervention can be a continuous pattern of *reacting to isolated incidents* rather than *developing a plan or approach* that will produce better *long term outcomes*. That is what this book is about.

There are as many approaches to teaching and educating children as there are people. Those approaches produce results ranging from satisfying and successful to frustrating and failing. Managing behavior for *any* student requires insight, keen observation, patience and lots of wisdom. Students who experience communication and learning difficulties frequently pose additional challenges. Some strategies that work for other students may be just as successful with our targeted population. However, since children with special needs may learn differently from their peers, the techniques for teaching and managing behavior frequently need to be modified.

In no way is this book attempting to offer a "cure" for all behavior problems. What it *will* do is identify a wide variety of behavior situations and problem behaviors that are related to communication; related to understanding, expression, or other learning skills such as establishing attention or memory. Once these specific situations are recognized, a variety of strategies will be offered. These techniques provide the support necessary to improve positive student participation. Considering the learning style of the targeted population, the focus of *visual strategies* to solve behavior problems is a natural consideration.

These are the links: ***behavior-communication-visual strategies***

- The *causes* of behavior differences are frequently related to communication difficulties; problems in understanding and/or difficulty with expression.

- The *remedy* to improve behavior is improving communication.

- The *method* is using visual strategies to support communication.

The development of *visually supported communication* or *visually mediated communication* strategies has evolved to be a significant source for improving communication for these students. Frequently, the improvement in behavior is directly related to improvement in communication; particularly the ability to understand. *Communication emerges as an integral part of the problem, or it evolves as an essential part of the solution.*

Solving Behavior Problems in Autism will begin with a short discussion of what we know about behavior. . . so author and readers will have a common starting place. There is no intention to try to exhaust the depth of knowledge on this subject. That would take volumes. Instead, a simple framework will be constructed so we can successfully explore that *behavior-communication-visual strategy*-link.

What is a behavior problem? What causes behavior problems? Historically, behavior management has produced a wide variety of approaches which all claim varying degrees of success or accomplishment. A brief summary of where we have been will help clarify the need for the focus on visual strategies.

Next we explore communication. Communication is more than "just speech." Many behavior programs miss that part. They focus on changing behavior. They target behaviors to be eliminated. It can become very clinical. The programs may not even accommodate for the communication needs of the student. If they do recognize the need to consider the student's communication abilities, the focus is usually on how well a student can *express* himself. Does he talk? Does he have an augmentative communication system? Although expression is a critically important skill, it is only a part, perhaps a small part, of the big picture. Communication is more complex than most people realize. There is more to understand. Behavior programs developed to provide logical, consistent structure for students will not achieve their maximum effectiveness if the student's communication skills are not considered. A deeper understanding of the communication process will help the reader look at behavior differently. This discussion is designed to add a few more pieces to that *behavior-communication-visual strategy* framework.

Any discussion of communication would not be complete without highlighting the use of visual strategies to improve communication. This is the third essential element in our framework. Understanding the immense impact of visual strategies on communication and behavior is the critical key. This book will build on the information presented in *Visual Strategies for Improving Communication Volume 1: Practical Supports for School and Home.* If you have not read that volume you will still benefit from this book. If you read Volume 1 you will gain even more insight, as well as tools and strategies to make a difference for your students.

The Individuals with Disabilities Act (IDEA) focuses on the provision of individualized programming and supports to enable students to participate successfully in school environments. The information in this book and the other books in the Visual Strategies Series provide excellent procedures to help that occur.

The information in this book has evolved as a result of years of experience working with students who have been given diagnostic labels such as autism, PDD, Asperger's Syndrome, autism spectrum disorder, emotional impairment, learning disability, attention deficit disorder, severe multiple impairment, cognitive impairment and others. Some of the most significant discoveries have occurred when developing programs for students with autism. Those students often represent the extremes of behavior difficulty, communication disorders and impairment in social skills. They can demonstrate the most confusing relationships between behaviors and their causes. What has been learned about that *behavior-communication-visual strategy* framework from working with those most challenged students has given us insight into programming for *all* students with special needs. As we devise strategies that work successfully with students with autism spectrum disorders, we are able to use those same techniques to effectively meet the needs of many students who need communication support. Please be creative as you apply this information to the individual students in your midst. Rather than focusing on a diagnostic label, identifying a student's *individual needs* will target numerous opportunities to use the information in this book to help the student achieve a higher level of success.

Once that *behavior-communication-visual strategy* framework is established, we will go on an adventure, discovering a multitude of ways that we can apply this information to real life situations. The rest of this book is designed to supply you with practical, easy-to-understand, easy-to-use strategies. One idea begets another. By the time you reach the end, you should have an abundance of ideas to pull out of your personal toolbox.

Part 1

THE LINK BETWEEN BEHAVIOR, COMMUNICATION AND VISUAL STRATEGIES

C h a p t e r
1

What Do We Know About Behavior?

By definition, everything we do is behavior. Smiling, eating, walking, and talking are behaviors. In early development, those behaviors are expected and encouraged. Most behavior is good, acceptable, appropriate. But that is not what people are thinking about when they talk about dealing with a student's "behavior." Behavior becomes a problem when we encounter situations where:

- students do not conduct themselves properly for the environment or situation

- their behavior does match not what we expect from their peers

- they do not do *what* we want them to do, *when* we want them to do it or *how* we want it done

Most behavior management programs begin with a system of analyzing situations to target specific behavior problems. Although that is an important step, this discussion will take a different path. When developing a framework for understanding behavior problems, it is helpful to begin by looking at what happens in the "normal" development of typical children. The focus on typical development will provide a reference point to help evaluate difficult behavior situations.

What do we know about child development?

OK. This is not where I was expecting you to begin. What does happen for most children? What is your version of "typical development?"

Babies are born cute (at least their parents think so), but not knowing a terrific amount about how we want them to act. Admittedly, even from the beginning, children are different from each other. They do not start out with the same raw material. Some pop out with compliant personalities and others emerge screaming and rebellious. After that, the course of development is even more unique for each. How a child develops and learns is directly related to many variables, including the expectations and demands of the environment he is growing up in and the parenting style of his primary caregivers. The key is that *every child is different.*

If every child is different, what are we supposed to understand?

As the child matures during the next twenty or so years, there will be zillions of things he needs to learn to become accepted, tolerated, socialized and enjoyed. Our goal is to raise a person who is productive and desirable to be with. When you objectively assess the adults you know, you will quickly understand that there is a wide range of "success" at the other end. What children become and what parents and teachers produce depends on so many variables that we could not even begin to count them. One of the greatest challenges for every parent and teacher is to discover the individual personality and "bent" of each child and then develop an effective style of mentoring that child to adulthood.

This is beginning to sound complicated. Where are you going with this?

Considering all the variables, "normal" development defies a simple definition. At the risk of adding to the confusion, there is one more piece to consider. Each child has a unique learning style: some are visual or auditory or tactile. Others need to be physically immersed in an activity to become engaged. Children learn at different speeds. While one child requires tough and consistent discipline, his playmate may respond to a parent's "look" and never consider engaging in an inappropriate behavior again.

How does a parent or teacher sort all this out?

That is the challenge. In one sense this seems complicated, however, there is also simplicity to the whole concept. Despite all the differences, there are some patterns and sequences of learning that are typical and expected for most children. From the first step of the toddler to the teenager's obsessive desire to possess the car keys and beyond, there are numerous developmental milestones that occur at fairly predictable ages. Here are a few to consider.

What are the milestones and behavior challenges in normal development?

Part of growing and maturing means hurdling childhood milestones. Some of those hurdles are classics in the "how to parent" section of the bookstore or library. That process of moving from total dependence on parents to developing enough skills to become an independent adult is a bumpy one. The goal is to gradually teach the skills that prepare students for more independence and autonomy. It is typical for behavior challenges to occur during these years while children are developing personal discipline, self-control, and decision-making skills.

Typical Challenges at Different Stages of Development

Sleep Problems: Cooperating with and following bedtime routines, getting in bed, going to sleep, staying asleep, and getting up in the night are common childhood challenges.

Eating Challenges: Many children experience strong preferences for certain foods and equally strong dislikes for others. Issues related to quantity of food consumed, quality of that food, timing of eating and the power struggles that can evolve around mealtimes are classic.

Terrible Two's: Children begin to learn the *power* of communication. Instead of using it just for social entertainment, they come to realize that they can actually manipulate some of their outside environment and control their destiny.

Toilet Training: For some children this is not an issue. For others it is a major undertaking. Parents and teachers have a high level of interest in students mastering this milestone.

Developing Responsibility: Taking care of personal belongings, following home or school rules and routines, developing dependability for performing tasks and responsibilities are all areas of challenge during the maturing process.

Social Skills: Developing the ability to play with peers, share, take turns, treat others respectfully, and participate in the various social routines necessary to "belong" to his social environment are essential skills to learn.

Self Control: Managing oneself in appropriate ways in areas of self discipline while experiencing a range of emotions from hurt and fear to anger and love can be some of the most difficult skills to master.

Physical and Sexual Development: Understanding body changes, adjusting to hormone variations and handling oneself in the related social challenges creates a unique set of problems.

Decision-Making: The ability to make acceptable choices and decisions is intertwined with intelligence, moral and spiritual training, and cultural factors. The student's family and social environment will greatly affect and define the parameters of success.

Developing Independence: Adolescence is a most challenging stage because the student's perception of what is appropriate behavior and acceptable independence is often in direct contradiction to the beliefs of parents and teachers. This conflict often affects other areas such as self-control, social skills, and responsibility.

Academic Achievement: Every step along the way is filled with multiple academic skills that parents and teachers want students to learn to prepare them for independent adulthood. The traditional reading, writing, and arithmetic are presented from a young age. Those academics are embellished with endless numbers of other skill areas and pieces of information that people deem important for students to master. Some students accomplish the learning eagerly and enthusiastically while others are uninterested or struggle to learn.

As students travel through this journey of milestones, they move from total *dependence on others* to gain some degree of *independence*. They move from having no intentional skills for controlling their environment to mastering the ability to get their wants and needs met. They acquire skills to negotiate social situations. They learn what styles of communication and behavior are acceptable in various environments. Understanding what *not* to say or do is a critical part of that learning curve. They discover which techniques work best to accomplish their purposes. Lots of learning. Lots of skills.

> *Like our typical kids, students with special needs are always developing new behaviors, both good and bad.*

What is different about students with special needs?

But children with special needs are different. How do you know what to expect from them?

Students who experience learning and developmental disabilities will encounter these same typical developmental challenges, however there may be major differences in their learning curves and timetables. As we focus on *children with special needs,* consider the following:

- Their development may be more *like* than *unlike* those developmental patterns of their normally developing peers.
- They may go through the same or similar developmental sequences as other children, but at *different speeds.*
- The timing of various developmental stages may match their *mental age* more than their *chronological age.*
- Some developmental stages may match their *chronological age* more than their *mental age.*
- They may *take longer to learn* appropriate behaviors or master skills.
- Their acquisition of skills may be *inconsistent* or reveal *uneven* development.
- Missing stages, missing skills or developing skills out of sequence may be observed.
- The instruction needed for them to learn and modify their behavior may be different from their peers.
- How the student accomplishes typical developmental milestones or learns specific skills may look different from other students because of his areas of disability and his learning style.
- Students may appear to stay at early developmental stages and not move on to more mature levels of behavior.
- They may *never* master some skills because of their specific cognitive or learning problems.

So what is the role of the parent or teacher during this maturing, developing process?

The role of parents and teachers is to *teach* the student what he needs to learn to move successfully through the stages of development to achieve independent adulthood. Parenting or teaching *any* child requires many skills. When the child you are teaching has some type of disability or special need, that job may become more complicated.

What makes raising and teaching the child with special needs so different from other students?

Because our expectations are continually challenged. We frequently don't know what to expect. *We need to engage in a continuous search to learn how the student's disability affects his ability.*

Good parenting is good parenting. Good teaching is good teaching. Students with special needs require teaching, training and correction, just like other students. The most effective parents and teachers *match their teaching style and expectations to the individual student.* This is important for all students, however, it becomes *critically* important when the student has special needs. It takes discernment to know how and when your strategies and expectations should be modified. The purpose of this book is to provide more support for that goal.

How does managing behavior problems fit into this discussion?

In the course of raising and teaching *all* students, there *will* be problems. That is inevitable. Students not doing what we want. Students doing things that are clearly inappropriate or unacceptable. Here is the problem: What is identified as a behavior problem and how it is handled depends on a multitude of variables.

- What one person considers a serious problem is not even noticed by another person.

- What presents an annoying difficulty at home or school may not be an issue at the other location.

- Expectations for student behavior may be different in various environments.

- Behaviors that are managed easily in familiar environments may create difficulties in new environments.

- People have many attitudes and opinions about behavior and what they consider problems.

- and lots more variables . . . .

> *We need to engage in a continuous search to learn how the student's **disability** affects his **ability**.*

How do you begin to sort out the behaviors you see so you can decide how to handle them?

When observing children who are demonstrating typical development, it becomes immediately obvious that there is a broad range of what is considered acceptable behavior. In addition, it becomes quite clear that there are some predictable reasons for students not doing what is expected. As children with *special needs* mature, they will experience many of the same challenges and milestones that their peers face. In addition, they will need to surmount some *additional challenges* resulting from the learning style differences, communication needs, and other individual deficiencies that result from their particular disability.

So that means students with special needs have to learn even <u>more</u> than their normally developing peers.

Yes, they can have more to learn. Not only are they struggling with the same challenges as their peers, they have more obstacles to overcome. Their difficulty is multiplied when you realize that their disabilities or special needs make it more difficult for them to do what their peers do. It is more difficult for them to learn what their peers are learning. Their challenges can be enormous.

I am beginning to feel overwhelmed. Where do you begin?

First, we need to look at a variety of reasons why behavior problems can occur. After identifying the causes or reasons for behavior differences, the solutions will evolve.

What are behavior problems?

- Two-year-old Billy climbs on Mom's lap and licks her cheek to "give her a kiss."
- Twenty-year-old, 250 pound Bill sits on Mom's lap and licks her cheek to "give her a kiss."

- Three-year-old Jessica reaches for her glass of milk, misses her target, and knocks over the glass, sending milk all over the table and carpet.
- Eight-year-old Jess sits with her arms folded. When she is told she can't have Coke for dinner she reaches out and whomps the glass of milk, sending it flying.

- Six-year-old Damien doesn't sit at the table for dinner. He wanders into the kitchen, picks up a piece of food and eats it while he wanders around the house.
- Five-year-old Dara will only eat French fries and pudding. . . nothing else.

- Four-year-old Christy tries to help Mom clear the dinner table. She drops the glass into the sink where it shatters to pieces.
- Nine-year-old Chris likes to bang on glasses with a spoon to make noise.

- Two-year-old Justin keeps pulling his shoes and socks off to run around barefoot.
- Eighteen-year-old Justin keeps pulling his shoes and socks off to walk around barefoot.

- Ten-year-old Sean bites the girl sitting next to him when she starts to cry.
- The girl starts to cry because she knows it makes Sean mad.

- Every time seven-year-old Kirsten goes into Wal-Mart she has a temper tantrum and cries until someone gets her a frozen drink to calm her down.
- Fourteen-year-old Benny puts his hands over his ears and yells when he goes into Wal-Mart.

- Three-year-old Mickey runs out of the bathroom with his pants around his ankles.
- Thirteen-year-old Mike runs out of the bathroom with his pants around his ankles.

- Six-year-old Danny throws toys when he gets mad.
- Sixteen-year-old Dan throws chairs when gets mad.

Behavior problems? Most people would think so.
Are some worse than others? Probably yes.
Are some age appropriate? Possibly.
Can they be changed or corrected? In most instances, yes.

The business of raising, teaching, and preparing children for adulthood contains incalculable opportunities to teach students new skills or correct their behavior. Growing and learning is a *process.* Teaching skills and changing children's behavior is a part of that process. There are an endless number of reasons why students do not do what we want them to do.

Does that mean that all behavior is not problem behavior?

Everything a child does is behavior. Some of it is purposeful and appropriate for meeting his needs and participating in his environment. Some of it occurs because the child is using all the strategies he knows how to use at that point in time to get his needs met. He hasn't learned what else to do. As children grow and mature they continue to naturally learn how to modify their actions so they become more effective at accomplishing their desires. Much of their learning is spontaneous. At times, however, they need specific instruction to guide them toward adjusting their actions to adult standards. No, all behavior is not a problem. All behavior is not bad.

But what do you call behavior problems? The title of this book is Solving Behavior Problems In Autism.

For the purposes of this book we will use a broad definition.

> *Behavior Problem:*
> *When a student is **not doing what I want** him or her to be doing*

or

> *Behavior Problem:*
> *When a student is **doing something I don't want** him or her to be doing*

For those who want a more specific description, consider these circumstances which usually cause concern:

- When a student's behavior is causing injury or harm to himself or others

- When a student's behavior prevents him from participating effectively in his life routines

- When a student uses behavior as an inappropriate or ineffective means of communicating

- When the student is engaging in behaviors or activities that are different from what is expected from him because of age, ability level, location, event, or activity

- When the student is not following or complying with the rules, routines, or expectations of specific occasions or environments

- When the student is not performing skills or engaging in actions or interactions effectively

- When the student is not performing his life routines at the level of independence expected for his age and ability level

- When a student does anything that calls attention to himself, making him significantly different from his peers

- When a student is doing anything that makes his parent or teacher "crazy"

There is a wide range of behaviors that will fit into that definition. Imagine the extremes:

On one end of the continuum are annoying habits and on the other end of the continuum are destructive behaviors that are injurious to the student himself or to others.

Annoying habits
Things that I want changed-
Really annoying behaviors
Behaviors that are causing problems
Behaviors that are causing really major problems
Behaviors that I can't stand any more
Behaviors that are preventing life routines
Behaviors preventing learning
Behaviors causing injury or destruction

Now, begin to place these behaviors on that continuum where you think they belong:

- flicking string
- whining
- picking his nose
- wetting his pants
- smearing feces
- taking off her shoes
- taking off his shirt
- taking off all her clothes
- eating his pencil eraser
- biting someone's arm
- eating too fast
- eating too much
- not eating
- spitting
- kicking
- saying "hi"
- saying "hi" fifty times
- crying
- throwing food
- hiding in a corner
- crying when you can't figure out what he wants
- having a temper tantrum in a store

- getting out of bed in the middle of the night
- running into the street
- climbing the fence
- touching the hallway walls
- looking at a fan
- searching for all the fans in the building
- looking at someone
- not looking at someone
- taking the furniture apart
- pulling down his pants
- leaving the bathroom before his pants are pulled up
- poking his fingers in your eyes
- touching buttons on the VCR
- asking the same question over and over
- saying things to other students that make them mad
- repeating what you said instead of answering your question

Many of these behaviors can be either a major or minor problem depending on the circumstances. Flicking a piece of string may be just an annoying fixation. It becomes a major problem if the student is packaging strings in craft kits and he destroys the kits by pulling the strings out. That string thing could become a huge social problem if the student pulls the strings out of other student's shoes or coats or sweat pants.

This list is just a beginning. Are you thinking about more behavior problems that are not on the list? Write them down so you can refer back to them later.

Some of the behaviors on your list don't seem like problems to me.

Good point! When we are defining what we consider behavior problems, there are lots of *variables*. Dealing with human behavior is different from the exact sciences. Remember that humans are all different and they bring those differences with them to any situation. What is considered a problem behavior for one child or by one adult may be considered acceptable in another situation. Let's consider some of the variables that determine what behavior is problem behavior.

What are the variables when identifying behavior difficulties?

When is a behavior a problem? Does the answer change? Are there different standards for different people or situations?

What we identify as a behavior problem changes depending on numerous variables. Who the student is, who the adult is and what environment they are in all play a part in whether specific behaviors are considered acceptable or not allowed. There are lots of variables that make it difficult to clearly define what a problem is. Think about how these elements affect our judgement.

• • • The Student • • •

We constantly alter our ideas about what behavior should be considered acceptable for different students.

- **Age:** Certain behaviors that are expected or acceptable in younger children are not tolerated when students get older.

Is It A Behavior Problem?
The Variables:

The Student

- age
- ability level
- communication skills
- social skills
- education level
- personality
- special needs

ME (the teacher or parent)

- childhood experiences
- education
- religious philosophy
- school policies
- personal control issues
- staff or family support
- expectations
- relationship with student
- life experience
- common sense

Environment

- home
- school
- community
  - eating
  - shopping
  - recreation
  - social traveling
  - work etc.

Educational Expectations

- curriculum
- educational goals
- peer groups

- **Ability Level:** Students can only perform at their level of ability. Actions generally match *cognitive* or *developmental* age rather than *chronological* age. Expecting students to act like their peers may not be realistic - particularly for students with more severe cognitive impairments. This should not be interpreted as an encouragement to accept immature or inappropriate behavior. It means that the ability level needs to be a critical consideration when determining what to expect from students.

- **Communication Skills:** Communication ability or disability is a variable that is frequently under-considered when evaluating behavior situations. It is often a significant factor in determining causes of problems and in developing solutions.

- **Social Skills:** How students understand and interpret social interactions and social information significantly affects how they manage their behavior.

- **Education Level:** The student's level of academic achievement will affect how they understand what is expected of them.

- **Personality**: Always remember that students have unique personalities that are independent of any special needs or disabilities they have.

- **Special Needs:** Each student is different and has unique needs. Some behaviors require additional consideration due to medical, emotional, physical or mental challenges. Other students are affected by perceptual or sensory differences. The challenge is to determine which unique needs *affect* his behavior and which unique needs *do not* need to alter our expectations for him.

• • • *The Parent and the Teacher* • • •

Each parent and teacher approaches a student from the perspective of his or her own life experiences. Their past history will determine their acceptance, tolerance, internal rules and the framework for their expectations from students. Here are some:

- **Their Own Childhood Experiences:** "When I was a child, this is what my parents did..."

- **Education:** Level of education and source of education greatly affect our perceptions of teaching and child rearing.

- **Religious Philosophy:** It frequently guides people's opinions, expectations, and techniques for managing difficulties.

- **School Policies:** How adults accept or reject the rules and structures that are established affects how they handle the students. How the school policies support the student's special needs influences how the adults can manage the students.

- **Personal Control Issues:** Adults range widely on this one. Some of them need to be "the boss" at all times. . . .they need to be "in control". Others believe in freedom. Some are afraid of exercising discipline. Others don't know how. Adults can be challenged when attempting to determine how much to support students and how or when to release them for independence.

- **Support from Others:** How much support is available from other staff members at school, or from family and friends at home, significantly affects how people cope with difficult behaviors.

- **Expectations:** Our expectations for typically developing students will skew our expectations for students with special needs. Our level of understanding the nature and impact of an individual student's disability will determine our success in mentoring that student.

- **Relationship with the Student:** How well we know the student, how thoroughly we understand his special wants and needs, how much we like that student and his nature all affect how we manage him.

- **Life Experience:** Experience in life; dealing with difficulties or challenges. Some adults are better at flexing or going-with-the-flow. The ability to think quickly, to adjust, to come up with creative options on the spot are skills where some adults are much more adept than others.

- **Common Sense:** We all approach challenging or unexpected situations by using what we know from our past experiences. Common sense (to us) guides our decision making. Of course, we know that everyone doesn't have the same common sense.

• • • *The Environment* • • •

- **Environmental Considerations:** Safety, noise level, activity level, other people, room arrangement and other factors will shape what we identify as behavior problems.

- **Expectations for Other People in the Location:** Each location has its unwritten rules of conduct. There are different levels of tolerance in different environments. The sports stadium or shopping mall tolerates different behavior than a church service. Gyms and hallways have different rules than the library.

• • • *Educational Expectations* • • •

- **Peer Group:** The student's peer group and our expectations for those peers will affect how we perceive what the student does.

- **Curriculum and Educational Goals:** How well the educational curriculum matches the student's needs and capabilities critically affects behavior. *How willing or able we are to adapt goals and expectations to meet his needs will determine how we perceive his performance.*

So how do these variables really affect behavior?

We need to remember that what is identified as a behavior problem and how it is handled is dependent on these and many more variables. What one person considers a serious problem is not even noticed by another person. A student's action presents a problem in one location, or with a specific person and is acceptable in another situation. So many variables. That's why there are such different opinions about what to work on and how to handle difficulties.

How do you sort through the variables to come up with effective ways of managing the students?

First, remember that because of the variables, *everyone involved will not see the situation the same way.*

Recognizing that we are viewing a problem from different vantage points helps us realize that we must first come to some common understanding about what we are viewing. One way to do that is to look more closely at the *causes* of behavior problems.

Why Do Behavior Problems Exist?

Dad took the family to the circus. Aaron was smiling as they got out of the car and walked to the area. When they entered the tent, Aaron began to pull Dad's arm and he screamed, "Eat! Eat!" Dad told Aaron it was not time for lunch yet. He tried to tell Aaron that the circus show was going to begin and they needed to get to their seats. Aaron pulled on Dad's arm. He sat down on the floor. His kicking and screaming could be heard over the commotion of the circus environment. Dad started yelling at Aaron to stop acting like that. He tried to hold Aaron. After a short while, Dad didn't know what else to do, so he ended up carrying Aaron back to the car to wait for the rest of the family.

Was Aaron "being bad" just to cause a problem? That is highly unlikely. The challenging question is: Why did Aaron have a problem? Unless we know the *cause* of his difficulty it will be extremely difficult to know how to avoid or to handle a problem like this. Here are some possibilities:

- Going to the circus was not a part of his normal routine and he did not know how to handle the new event.

- Going to the circus was so exciting to Aaron that his excitement escalated to a point of being out of control.

- Aaron did not know what to expect at the circus and when he saw strange and different things, he was afraid.

- Going into the circus tent reminded Aaron of the amusement park where he had a problem a few months ago.

- The environment was too noisy or smelly. Perhaps it was too hot or the flashing lights annoyed him.

- When Aaron yelled "Eat! Eat!" he may have been physically hungry.

- Perhaps Aaron yelled "Eat! Eat!" because he saw the popcorn vendor.

- Yelling "Eat! Eat!" could have been a way of saying he had a stomach ache.

- Aaron may have been trying to communicate what was *really* bothering him but the words "Eat! Eat!" were the only words that would come out. He didn't have the language to tell Dad what the problem really was.

- Once Aaron was expressing his difficulty, his behavior just escalated. He didn't know how to stop. He didn't know how to calm down.

> *The most critical step in attempting to solve behavior problems is to identify **why** the behavior difficulties exist.*

I can think of some other possible reasons for Aaron's problem!

It's great if you can add to the list of possible reasons for Aaron's difficult trip. *The most critical step in attempting to solve behavior problems is to identify **why** the behavior difficulties exist.* Perhaps there was one cause for Aaron's problem. It is more likely that a combination of issues created the escalation of Aaron's behavior. Once we identify why the student is behaving in a particular way, we will have the most important information we need to enable us to change something to help solve the problem.

Why do behavior problems exist?

I wish we knew all the answers to this question. There are endless numbers of reasons that we may never know. In spite of that, there are lots of predictable reasons that will cause difficulty. Let's discuss some of the common categories of reasons that our students will encounter problems. Of course these lists are not all inclusive, but they should get your thinking stimulated. Once we target the reasons we will use that information to solve the problems.

What are common causes of behavior problems?

WHO THE STUDENT IS:

Some behavior problems evolve because of who the student is. He is a unique "package", unlike any other. The way he responds to the world will be different from anyone else, based on his own individual circumstances. Behavior will be shaped by who he or she is.

■ Age or Developmental Level:

Some behavior difficulties are naturally associated with stages of development. Remember that students with special needs will encounter the same types of problems as their peers, only the *timing* of their challenges will probably match their *developmental* level rather than their *chronological* age.

Example: Twelve-year-old Justin keeps putting everything in his mouth. Because of his severe mental impairment, Justin is functioning at the six to twelve month stage of development. Mouthing things is a typical or normal behavior for children in the six to twelve month age range. Although Justin's behavior is not appropriate for a twelve-year-old, it matches his developmental level.

Example: Five-year-old Stephanie is just emerging in her ability to communicate. She is beginning to take a person by the hand to get something she wants. She is learning to use some gestures to request or protest. She can now say three words: potty, pretzels, and NO. Stephanie has started to protest all the time. Whatever someone wants her to do, she very clearly communicates NO. Although it may appear that sweet Stephanie's personality has changed, the real problem is that she has probably entered that "terrible two" stage. The "terrible two's" are a time when children are beginning to learn the power of communication and how to make it work to get their wants and needs met. It appears that is exactly what is happening for Stephanie.

You may observe that students with special needs will require more time or more support to accomplish normal childhood milestones. Because of some of the other causes for behavior problems on this list, their difficulty with the childhood milestones may be much more severe than those of other children. Managing them through the problem times may take a lot more effort than for other children.

Causes of Behavior Problems

Who The Student Is

- age
- developmental level
- disability/special needs
- interests
- family issues
- childish misbehavior
- learning style
- temperment
- personality

What Student Can Do

- communication skills
- social skills
- learned behavior
- skills or deficits related to disability
- functional skills

Where The Student Is

- environment
  - physical environment
  - functional environment
- other people

Related Issues

- sensory differences
- medical needs

Typical Developmental Milestones with Behavior Challenges:

- sleeping
- eating
- play skills
- "terrible two's"
- toilet training
- following the rules
- cleaning the bedroom
- skills for independence
- curfew
- "terrible teens"
- Etc. etc. etc.

■ **Family Issues:**

It's hereditary! Sometimes our children act more like us than we would want. It is common to hear, "He acts just like _____!" Then you fill in the blank with the name of a parent or sibling, a grandparent or some other relative. Sometimes a child is so different from the rest of the family than no one knows how to cope. Behavior expectations and the style of parenting within a family can actually cause behavior problems or at least reinforce them.

Family Patterns that Can Cause Behavior Problems:

- parenting skills
- family communication styles
- inconsistent discipline
- ineffective discipline
- inconsistent expectations between parents
- inappropriate expectations for a child
- acceptance or rejection of the child's special needs
- dynamics with multiple children
- family life style
- structure or lack of structure in the home
- routines or lack of routines in the home
- expectations because of cultural differences
- adhering to "what my parents used to do (or not do)"
- major family challenges or problems of other family members
- other family issues that may not appear to have any relationship to the student

> *Remember, sometimes kids are "just a chip off the old block." They are more like us than we realize. Perhaps they are more like us than we want them to be. We may become more intolerant of those things that they do that are similar to our own personal challenges.*

WHAT THE STUDENT CAN DO:

How the student handles situations in his life is totally dependent on what skills he has. . . what he has to work with. All students do not have the same tools to work with. Think about these major areas.

■ Communication and Social Skills:

For students with autism and other students who experience mild to severe communication disabilities, communication difficulties can be a *primary* reason for many behavior problems. Communication involves a collection of complex skills that interweave to produce effective action and interaction. It is critical to remember that *communication is more than just speech.*

Understanding the communication of others, trying to figure out what is happening or not happening, handling changes and transitions, and interpreting cues and signals in the environment can all be areas of difficulty for this population. These students can experience significant difficulty effectively *expressing* themselves. Whether they are verbal or non-verbal, the strategies these students use to get their wants and needs met and to interact socially with others may not work efficiently. *Inappropriate behaviors may actually work more effectively for a student than other forms of communication.* Understanding why communication problems exist and where communication breakdowns contribute to behavior difficulties is a significant step toward developing successful solutions.

Areas of Communication Breakdown that Contribute to Behavior Problems:

Comprehension:
- Students don't understand what is happening or what is expected of them.
- They inaccurately interpret what they see or hear.
- They misunderstand or misinterpret social information and social attempts of others.
- Student difficulty in establishing attention results in missing information or not being able to follow ongoing activity.
- Delay in processing information reduces their ability to participate effectively.

Expression:
- Lack of effective gestures, facial expressions, body language or communication supports hinders ability to communicate information.
- Inability to produce intelligible speech with appropriate, effective use of vocabulary affects ability to express clear ideas.
- Inappropriate response to social interactions creates difficulty participating in conversations.

Social/Pragmatic Skills:
- Impairment in establishing, maintaining and shifting attention reduces effective communication.
- Difficulty staying involved in a social interaction reduces appropriate social connection.
- Not taking turns appropriately in social exchanges results in inappropriate social interactions.
- Difficulty recognizing communication breakdowns makes communication ineffective.
- Lack of skills for repairing communication breakdowns causes frustration when they don't get their wants and needs met.

> *When students are trying to get their needs met, inappropriate behavior may work better than other forms of communication.*

Students need to effectively perform many skills to accomplish effective communication interactions. Behavior problems emerge because students don't understand. They will do what they think they are supposed to do.

Students will use whatever means they can to accomplish their intents. Frequently, undesirable behaviors are used because they produce more response from others than other communication forms. Problem behavior or inappropriate behavior frequently works better than other impaired communication attempts.

■ **Learning Style Differences:**
Student behavior is influenced by individual learning differences that affect how they are able to perform in whatever situations they are in. Learning style differences affect how much the student learns and how rapidly he learns effective skills to replace inappropriate behaviors.

Individual Differences that Affect Student Behavior:
- Intellectual ability
- Rate of learning
- Learning disabilities
- Level of distractibility
- Memory skills
- Learning strengths and weaknesses

> *Occasionally students with autism have unusual or peculiar ways of understanding or interpreting their environment. Perhaps the cues that they are focusing on are not the cues that the rest of the world would most likely pay attention to. Their* **idiosyncratic** *way of understanding may not be easy to interpret. The result is students who respond to situations in peculiar or unusual ways. They are not being bad. They are just not seeing the same big picture that you and I are seeing.*

■ Lack of Generalization of Learned Skills:

What we learn from one experience gets stored into our brains in a "storage data base." When we become involved in another situation, our brains go back to the data base to see if there are any similarities or if something was learned in the first situation that will have application for handling the second situation. Some students with disabilities, particularly those with autism, are observed to experience considerable difficulty generalizing learning from one situation or setting to another.

■ Learned Behavior:

Many times students behave in certain ways because that is how they learned to handle specific situations. We may consider the behavior inappropriate or problematic, however, the student has somehow been reinforced to use these actions to get their wants and needs met. It is not unusual for adults to respond to students by actually rewarding undesirable behavior. Once students learn behaviors like these, they can be difficult to change.

Learned Behavior that Causes Difficulty:

1. Learned Helplessness: Without realizing it we can teach students to be dependent on us to do things for them. The principle that is sometimes difficult for us to remember is: If we do it for them, they don't need to learn to do it for themselves. This is as true for the college student with dirty laundry as it is for the two-year-old learning to put on his socks.

2. Learned Dependency: We can teach skills and routines in ways that require our prompting to be a part of the routine-forever. Students may learn that our prompt is a form of "turn-taking" that becomes integrated into the learned routine. What the student learns to do is take a turn by performing one step of the routine and then wait until we take our turn of prompting them before they perform the next step of the routine.

THE FAMILY CIRCUS®

5-13
©1993 Bil Keane, Inc.
Dist. by Cowles Synd., Inc.

"When somebody gives you something, you wait for them to say, 'And what do you say?' Then you say 'Thank you.'"

3. Learned Chains of Behavior: For as much as it is said that our targeted students have difficulty learning, sometimes they learn a series of behaviors - a chain of behaviors - where one behavior gradually escalates to another behavior which escalates to another, eventually leading to a full-blown incident. These situations can become a significant challenge because once a chain begins it may be difficult to interrupt or change the student's behavior to keep him from completing the escalation throughout the entire chain.

4. Learned Routines: If we don't teach them a routine to accomplish a task, they will develop their own routine. The problem results when the routine that they develop is not appropriate or efficient. Once their routine is established, it is difficult to make changes. Consequently, it is better to make sure that new tasks are learned in appropriate sequences. It is also prudent to teach tasks and routines with a long-term view so students won't have to spend valuable time unlearning behavior appropriate only for younger children and then relearn more mature behavior as they get older.

5. Learned Responses: As students react to specific significant events, they may repeat that same behavior or response every time the memory of that event is repeated. This can be particularly obvious when they react strongly to something that they perceive as frightening or highly undesirable. Even though the surrounding factors may change, they may still react strongly every time that event is triggered. Example: Several years ago he saw a dog that frightened him so much that he cried. Now he cries every time he sees a dog.

6. Learned by Imitation: Students imitate each other. They imitate the adults around them. Why is it that they don't learn what we want them to and then they imitate what we do not want them to learn? It seems like they don't learn the good stuff and they do learn what we consider bad.

*Currently, one of the critical controversies in education is inclusion. The question is: Will a child with special needs learn better by being integrated into a regular education setting with normally developing peers, or will he fare better with programming in some type of specialized setting? At the crux of this issue is determining how much a student will learn just by being in an environment. How much will he pick up "by osmosis"? Particularly for students with autism, just being present in an environment may not be enough. Because of the nature of the disability, these students frequently need to be **specifically taught** the skills that we want them to learn. That is not to suggest that they will not learn by imitation. Imitation is one of the ways that they may develop skills, depending on their individual ability level. What happens, however, is that since they do not have the same sense of social discrimination that other students have, they may not be very discerning about which skills to imitate. They cannot distinguish which things are good to imitate and which things are considered bad or will get them into trouble. It is not unusual for them to imitate other student's most dramatic behaviors that have caused noticeable response, for example, swearing or talking back to the teacher.*

WHERE THE STUDENT IS:

The environment plays a significant role in how a student handles his behavior. The environment a student is in can be the factor that can totally change his behavior by taxing his coping skills. Think about these issues.

■ The Physical Environment:

Every environment that a student is in presents unique challenges. Adjusting to the built-in elements can be extremely difficult. It is not unusual for a student's behavior to change in different places. Various locations provide challenge because of some physical quality. Students must learn to adjust their behavior to match where they are.

The Environment: Typical Physical Elements that Create Opportunities for Behavior Problems

- sensory overload
- physical space - too big or too small
- location of materials
- location of temptations
- who is there
- seating arrangements
- size of the chair
- visual distractions
- building logistics

■ The Functional Environment:

Functioning within different environments can be difficult for students because of the changing rules and expectations. In school, a student who is highly successful in one classroom can totally fall apart in a different class. There is much in the community that is not supportive or adjustable. The behavior problems emerge as a result of a lack of skills to compensate for the differences.

The Environment: Functional Challenges that Cause Behavior Difficulties

- communication systems; communication support
- pace, confusion, structure
- instructional style
- changes and transitions
- expectations for behavior
- expectations for independence
- rules and routines that are unfamiliar or that change
- how the student is able to participate in ongoing activities
- social demands
- behavior of other students
- how other people accommodate for the student
- instructional content
- how the ongoing curriculum matches the student's ability
- how the ongoing activity matches the student's interests
- options for flexibility
- extra support a student receives or does not receive
- nothing for the student to do

■ The Social Environment:

We focus on the student whose behavior is not acceptable. We pay attention to what he or she does that is inappropriate. We notice when he fails to do what is expected. In honest assessment, *sometimes the behavior problems are really caused by other people. What the other people are doing or not doing is the real presenting problem.* Our targeted student is simply responding or reacting in the ways he knows. Perhaps his responses are inappropriate or his communication skills do not adequately handle the situation, but the *true cause* of the difficulty is other people. This is not an attempt to suggest blaming others for the student's behavior difficulties. It is necessary, however, to view the student in the context of the people around him.

The Environment: Ways Other People Cause the Student to Exhibit Behavior Problems

- Not responding to the student's communication attempts
- Not communicating to the student in a *form* he can understand
- Not being an effective communication partner
- Not responding appropriately to the student's sensory needs: i.e. not wanting to be touched, needing personal space, difficulty with noise levels or area lighting
- Having unrealistic or inappropriate expectations for the student
- Intentionally or thoughtlessly putting students in situations they will handle inappropriately
- Teasing
- Not accommodating for the student's special needs

RELATED ISSUES:

Many students demonstrate behavior difficulties because of other specific needs that are not well defined. Even though related areas can significantly affect behavior, they are frequently undiagnosed or not addressed. These issues are common in autism and occur regularly in students with other special needs.

■ Sensory Differences:

Sensory input refers to the information our bodies gain from our senses. We gain information from:

- sight
- sound
- touch
- smell
- taste
- motion (also known by terms such kinesthia, proprioception, or vestibular sensation)

Sensory differences are common in students with special needs. These students may be overly sensitive (hyper-reactive) and/or under sensitive (hypo-reactive) to various kinds of sensory stimuli. Although this dysfunction will be observed in people in the regular population, there is a significantly higher number of students with autism who experience sensory differences than in the general population. This is a complex problem, caused because something is not working correctly in the nervous system.

It is common for these students to engage in a variety of behaviors in an attempt to increase or reduce their sensory stimulation so they will become more comfortable. Some behaviors may be persistent or excessive repetitions of actions that are considered fairly normal. Other behaviors might reach extreme or bizarre proportions. Once you understand that a student has sensory differences or sensory extremes, it can help explain some of the behaviors you may observe. For example, rocking, spinning or flapping hands may be an attempt to provide more stimulation to the brain. Hands over the ears (because it is too noisy), ripping clothing (because it feels funny on my body) or not sitting by a certain person (because of the strange smell of their cologne) may be attempts to reduce over stimulation to the brain.

Students who do not have the communication skills or self-management skills to get their sensory needs met in acceptable ways are likely to cause major disruptions or perplexing situations.

Typical Behavior Differences Caused by Sensory Needs

- Ron wraps himself tightly in his shirt, preventing him from using his hands to do his work
- David only eats only pudding, peanut butter and bread
- Meg walks in an odd way with her shoulder up and her head tilted
- Jerry constantly plays with his saliva
- Patty frequently puts her hands over her ears

> *Sorting out behaviors caused by sensory needs is a complicated task. Working with an Occupational Therapist who is knowledgeable about the sensory needs of this population is critical for thoroughly understanding the unique profile of an individual student.*

There are occasions where a child's different behavior is the result of a vision problem or a hearing problem. If he can't see or he can't hear well he will not perform well. Sometimes the obvious is not recognized.

■ Medical Needs:

There is growing acknowledgment that a higher percentage of students with special needs have co-occurring medical problems than in the normal population. That means some students who have a diagnosis of autism or some other developmental disability may also have other medical conditions. It is surprising how many of these students have not had the benefit of a thorough medical evaluation. This is not to suggest that medical treatment will "cure" the autism. But it does suggest that some of the difficulties the student is experiencing may be related to something other than autism.*

Typical Medical Conditions Related to Behavior Problems:

- seizure disorders
- anxiety disorders
- mood disorders: depression/bipolar /obsessive compulsive disorders
- sleep disorders
- ADD/ADHD
- allergies
- nutrition problems
- vision or hearing impairments
- dental needs
- common childhood illnesses
- recurring infections
- PMS

*(As of this writing, the medical field is investigating numerous possible causes and treatments for autism. Although there are hopeful discoveries emerging, there is no common specific medical treatment at this time.)

Student behavior, participation and performance can be significantly affected by medical needs. Imagine how you perform when you don't feel well or when you are tired. Medical treatment will often change co-occurring medical difficulties, which will alter the student's behavior patterns. Be alerted. There is much confusion regarding this topic. There are times when medical issues are addressed unrealistically. At one extreme is searching for the "magic cure". At the other extreme is ignoring treatable conditions. Keep these thoughts in mind:

- Medical intervention can dramatically change student behavior by controlling, reducing or eliminating co-occurring physical problems.

- In some unique cases there are medical discoveries and treatments that create dramatic changes in students. These results would be directly related to the specific causes of that student's physical and neurological condition. Since there are many different causes for student disabilities, there is no one treatment that has been proven to work for all students.

- Medical treatment is not a "cure" for a developmental disability.

- Addressing medical needs does not replace the need for teaching appropriate skills to the student.

- Teaching communication skills and making environmental adjustments will not replace the need for appropriate medical intervention.

The bottom line when talking about behavior is that student behavior can frequently be affected by some medical need the student has. Addressing the student's medical needs can assist in producing changes in the student's overall behavior. Remember that each student is different and treatment requires a specific individualized approach.

There are currently many areas of medical exploration investigating causes and effective treatments that are showing significant promise for people with autism spectrum disorders. Finding medical support from someone who understands the unique needs of children with disabilities, particularly with autism, is important. Because of their poor communication skills and their unique behavior patterns, these students are more difficult to evaluate. The solutions to some of their medical needs are not simple. Knowledge about emerging medical discoveries related to this population will affect treatment decisions.

■ Childish Misbehavior:

Never forget that kids are kids and sometimes they do things just because.

Typical Childish Misbehaviors include:

- exploring
- experimenting
- testing the rules
- rebellion
- making mistakes
- having accidents

WOW!!! There are a lot of reasons why behavior problems exist!

Now you can understand why one behavior management technique does not fit all situations.

Example: Mark is running around and tearing his shirt because the tag in the back is bothering him. He doesn't have the communication skills to tell Mom what the problem is. Timing him out or forcing him to "do his work" will not solve the problem. In fact, those interventions may actually make the situation worse. When Mark gets frustrated because the original problem is continuing, his behaviors may actually escalate as he tries to change the problem that he has.

It is not realistic to think that we will always be able to diagnose why a student's behavior is a problem. Sometimes the reason may actually be multiple reasons. But taking the time and energy to explore the possible causes of the problems our students encounter will help create a framework for understanding that will significantly affect the success of any attempts to change the problem behaviors.

Considering this discussion about why behavior problems exist, it will be helpful to look at the history of behavior management. There have been a variety of approaches used with varying degrees of success.

Behavior Management 101

The history of behavior management has produced a wide variety of approaches, many controversial, which all claim varying degrees of success or accomplishment. It seems that all the approaches have worked somehow for someone. This is an area that produces strong attitudes and opinions about which approaches are appropriate and how success is defined.

Historically, there have been several major philosophical approaches to behavior management. Major areas of study have included:

- **Biophysical:** medications, vitamin therapies, diets

- **Psychodynamic:** psychological therapy, counseling

- **Sociological**: focusing on developing social relationships

- **Ecological:** examining and changing the environment or other people

- **Behavioral:** providing data based teaching structure to change behavior, i.e. behavior modification, applied behavior analysis

- **Sensory:** providing activities or environmental modifications to increase or reduce sensory stimulation

- **Skill-based:** teaching specific skills to improve functioning and performance

- **Communication-based:** teaching communication skills necessary to get wants and needs met

Each approach has produced a positive outcome for some students, depending on the cause of their behavior problems. No approach solves all behavior problems.

Historically there has been little attention aimed toward assessing how a student's ability to understand and interpret communication relates to the behaviors he exhibits.

The most successful programs to support students and solve behavior problems are frequently eclectic combinations of several different strategies and approaches.

What is the best behavior management approach to use?

It is not within the scope of this book to support or reject any specific behavior programs. As you can see, any of these approaches have the potential to help some students, depending on the *cause* of their specific behavior problems. The techniques in this book, emphasizing the development of improved communication, will support any well designed educational or behavior management program. Using visual strategies to improve student understanding and expression is an approach that can be integrated into most interactions with students.

I have been investigating. . . looking for answers. It's confusing! How do you sort through it all?

When you are looking for answers to the behavior challenges you are facing, it can feel like you are on a shopping trip. It can feel like intervention approaches are advertised like new cars. Many of those programs are intimidating because they are filled with technical vocabulary that is not easily understood. Sometimes people are heard claiming their choice. . .. "We are using the Smith approach." or "They are doing the Jones program." It begins to sound like making the program choice is the goal. . . the end. Once that is done, the process is complete. Some of these people find success. Others become embroiled in frustration. It is important not to "jump on the bandwagon" of the "popular therapy of the day" without carefully identifying what the student's needs are and what you hope to accomplish.

Why doesn't choosing a system fix things? Isn't that what needs to be done? Isn't that what we are trying to do?

Dealing with behavior problems is more complicated than that. We need to remember that our students with special needs are human beings. *They are children with some body systems that are not working totally correctly.* They handle life in ways that make sense to them. They use the skills that they have to use. They behave in the ways that they know to accomplish their purposes. That is behavior. Sometimes the behavior they use is considered appropriate and acceptable. At other times their behavior is unsatisfactory. It needs to be changed. When it needs to be changed, we usually need to do something to help it to change.

You are starting to make this sound too simple. Are you trying to confuse me?

There is a simple way to look at behavior management. The early pioneers in the field of psychology spent a lot of time observing both animals and people to study how behavior occurs and how it changes. One of their major discoveries was that making changes in the environment resulted in changes in their subject's behavior.

Here are some simple observations that are modified to apply to our discussion.

1. When a student uses a behavior that works to accomplish his goal, he will use that behavior over again.

2. When a student uses a behavior to try to accomplish a purpose and it does not work, he will try something different.

3. If we want a student to change a behavior that she is doing, *something needs to change.*

4. A way to make a student's behavior change is to create change. A plan can:

   • change how things are being presented to the student
   • modify what the student is reacting to or responding to
   • adjust what is expected of the student
   • teach students different ways to respond or react
   • determine what actions should be rewarded, reinforced, or encouraged

This, of course, is a simplistic explanation. But the bottom line is to recognize that *to get a student to change his behavior, something needs to change.* Very often, that change needs to occur in us or needs to be created by us. That is where the problem occurs. It is easy to focus on the need for the student to change. We don't like to think about looking at ourselves.

Do you mean that <u>I</u> have to change so the student will change?

That is a possibility. An effective behavior program will help you sort out what needs to be changed. You may need to:

   • change how you communicate to the student
   • alter how you respond to what he is doing
   • modify something in the environment
   • or, a zillion other possibilities

You may need to make a change in your own behavior or you may need to facilitate some kind of change in the environment.

> *Students will do what makes sense to them. They will use what works to accomplish their goals.*

> *Think about how this old saying applies to our discussion:*
> **IF YOU DO WHAT YOU ALWAYS DID. . . YOU'LL GET WHAT YOU ALWAYS GOT.**

> *This, of course, is a simplistic explanation. But the bottom line is to recognize that to get a student to change his behavior, something needs to change. Very often, that change needs to occur in us or needs to be created by us. That is where the problem occurs. It is easy to focus on the need for the student to change. We don't like to think about looking at ourselves.*

Well, how do you know what to change?

That depends on the *cause* of the problem. One of the goals in any assessment is to decide what needs to change. In order to do that, you need to identify what you think the cause of the problem is. Once you identify the cause, you can create solutions that will provide the support necessary to alter the student's behavior.

The *most effective* behavior plans and approaches achieve success because they:

- focus on identifying the *causes* of behavior problems rather than attempting to change the child's external behaviors without considering *why* they are occurring
- *do not presume that students understand communication or social situations*
- are sensitive to the student's learning style differences so the student's *learning strengths are maximized*
- *teach skills in the context of real life situations* to maximize generalization of positive behaviors into life routines
- recognize that dealing with human beings is different from dealing with machines. . . there is always a human element

What's missing in behavior intervention for students with autism?

Many behavior intervention strategies seem to miss the mark with students who have autism spectrum disorders. Too often, behavior is addressed without understanding the *causes* of the behavior or addressing the *critical underlying deficits that cause the behavior.* You cannot truly understand the behavior of students with autism without understanding the nature of autism.[1]

Research is pointing to differences in various parts of the brain. This affects how students with autism perceive the world around them and how they attempt to respond to those perceptions. If a student *mis-perceives,* he is likely to *mis-respond.* Then it is easy for the people working with that student to *mis-interpret* the behavior. They may attribute it to:

conscious intent	*doing it on purpose*	(which *can* be modified)
	rather than	
organicity	*the result of differences in the brain*	(which *cannot* be modified)

The consequence is behavior interventions that yield unsuccessful or disappointing results.

Some behavior challenges occur with *all* children during normal growth and development. Those behavior problems can be the result of inadequate learning or the child's attempts to test the limits. They occur when children are tired or hungry or when they are told they can't have what they want. Occasionally children demonstrate willful defiance in an attempt to find out how much power and control they really have over other people. Students with autism and those with other disabilities may demonstrate these same types of developmental behavior difficulties as their peers.

The behavior challenges of students who have special needs can be significantly more complex than those of other children. Autism frequently represents the extremes in behavior difficulties. These students have behavior problems for *different reasons* than their peers. There are *different causes* for their difficulties. Difficulty with communication is a root of many problems. The differences in their brains affect:

- how they *perceive* the environment
- how they are able to *understand and interpret* communication and social interaction
- how they are able to *express* themselves to get their wants and needs met and participate in social interactions

Traditional approaches to managing behavior problems often prove ineffective because they do not accommodate for these student's differences. Without understanding how students with autism spectrum disorders learn and *how* they understand, our behavior management approaches will never truly succeed.

I am beginning to understand, but how do you make changes? What changes are necessary? What is most important?

Communication becomes a significant issue. Communication is frequently identified as a *cause* of behavior difficulties. In addition, communication evolves as a valuable resource when attempting to solve the difficulties. Regardless of what behavior plan you implement, the student's communication ability needs to be a *critical* consideration. The success or failure of any teaching approach depends on the accurate assessment of an individual student's communication skills. Students will achieve maximum potential when there is accommodation for their communication needs. Using their learning strengths to teach needed social and communication skills and appropriate behavior will accomplish the most success. Understanding more about communication will tie this all together.

> *If we focus so intently on the* **program** *that we lose sight of the* **student***, we won't gain much.*

Chapter 2

Understanding Communication

There are a number of terms that are used such as cognitive ability, intellectual capacity, IQ, or intelligence, to describe the student's mental ability or capacity to learn. The development of communication skills will usually parallel the student's overall level of development.

Communication is more than "just speech." The development of communication is a more complicated process than most people comprehend. From that first cry at birth, there are multiple biological and neurological systems that unfold. Early cognitive development involves the maturing of sensory processes, perception, memory and numerous skills that lead to thinking, reasoning and problem solving. Intertwined in the development of cognition are numerous skills that eventually evolve into communication.

How does a child learn to communicate?

In normal development, the process of emerging communication just seems to unfold. There is evidence that children are predisposed or prewired to attend to language and to communicate with the people around them. Within days and weeks from birth, babies begin to demonstrate that they have preferences for certain sounds and voices. In those first few months of life, they develop the ability to smile, interact with people around them and vocalize a repertoire of sounds. Their early communication skills appear to emerge in part from an internal time clock that sets the process in motion. Skill development is enhanced and encouraged through their naturally occurring exposure to people and experiences. Social play is an important part of this development. Parents across cultures seem to know instinctively how to interact with their infants to foster the emergence of these skills.

What about speech? How does speech develop?

As their babies grow, parents watch for the common markers of successful development: social play, the child's ability to understand communication, and his or her development of verbal language. Their primary attention is focused on the child's first words. In fact, those first words are so exciting that they are recorded in baby books along with other developmental milestones.

Typically developing children learn to understand language, express their wants and needs and engage in social interactions with others. Speech begins with one-word utterances and two word combinations and grows to the point where complex conversations are prevalent. Most of these skills develop naturally from the interaction between a child and his environment. A child masters numerous skills to eventually become a competent communicator.

But some children don't develop speech, or if they do develop speech it seems very different. Help me understand this.

Some children do not acquire communication skills following the normal developmental timetable. Children who are *delayed* in communication development learn skills much slower than their age mates do. Other children are *disordered* in their acquisition of communication skills. Those children seem to do things very differently. Not only can they be slow in developing skills, but what they do learn is different, unusual or doesn't work very well. Before trying to explain what can go wrong with communication development, it is necessary to explain in more detail what is supposed to happen.

How do early communication skills develop?

Even though most people are acutely aware of the first words of young children, there are many other skills and awarenesses that emerge prior to and simultaneously with those first words. This is such a complex process that it could take a whole book to discuss the details. What is important to understand is that there are other skills besides speech that are critically necessary for a child to become an effective communicator.

> *The better that people understand the dynamics of communication, the more effectively they will be able to interact with and manage the behavior of students with autism spectrum disorders.*

> *Because communication is intertwined so intricately with cognition, students who are cognitively delayed will most likely demonstrate a delay in the development of communication skills that parallels their intellectual ability. That does not mean that all students who are delayed in developing communication skills are cognitively delayed (mentally impaired). Slow development of communication skills can occur for a variety of reasons.*

Imagine the major challenge a baby has as he enters the world of communication. As he sees and hears all the stimuli coming in, he somehow has to evaluate it, categorize it, and make sense of it. He needs to figure out what to remember and realize what to discard. He needs to grasp that the voice of a person is different from the squeak of a door. He has to derive meaning from all the actions and language of the people around him. As he hears and begins to understand language, he needs to build a massive filing cabinet in his brain to help him store and remember what it all means.

But I want my child to talk. Speech is important. Isn't that enough?

No, just producing speech is not enough. Rather than detail every step of normal development, in the context of this book, it will help to discuss some of the types of skills children develop.

Understanding is an essential beginning to communication. Children begin developing skills to help them *understand* the social interactions of others. The methods or *forms* of communication that other people use to interact with the child begin to make sense to him. Children begin to interpret:

- the sound of someone's voice
- facial expressions
- gestures
- touch
- movement
- body language
- objects or items that are a part of communication
- specific words a person uses
- vocal intonation patterns

As children become engaged in those first social interactions, they begin to respond. Long before speech develops, children acquire many other *preverbal* skills to enable them to interact with people. *Preverbal communication* is accomplished by using gestures, body movements, eye contact and other non-speech skills. These skills are essential beginnings to really effective communication. *Preverbal* communication skills include:

Socialization:
- seeking attention
- looking at someone to establish a social connection with them
- looking at the same object with another person so they are sharing in the experience (joint attention)
- staying involved in social interactions

Social Turn-Taking:
- social turn-taking with another person
- responding when someone is trying to interact with them
- playing back-and-forth social games (like peek-a-boo)

Communicative Intent:
- intentionally doing something to get a response from another person

- using gestures, vocalizations, or some other means to let you know what he wants or doesn't want

As these communication purposes are developing, children gradually use a variety of methods or *forms* to communicate their wants and needs.

Forms of Communication:
- natural gestures:
  - reaching
  - touching
  - pointing
  - pushing away
  - waving
  - smiling
  - nodding his head
  - shaking her head

HELP!

These skills emerge quite early in children who are developing communication skills along a normal timetable. When children are delayed in acquiring speech they may also be delayed or disordered in acquiring these related communication skills.

- vocalizations *(not speech yet):*
  - crying, screaming
  - grunts and sounds
  - producing different vowel and consonant sounds

- body language:
  - taking a person by the hand somewhere
  - moving closer or farther from a person (changing proximity)
  - facial expressions
  - establishing eye contact

- using props or supports:
  - giving or showing something
  - objects
  - pictures or photographs
  - printed matter, written language

It is obvious that some of the early forms of communication that children use to express their wants and needs are more acceptable than others.

Have you have ever had the experience of going to an environment where everyone is speaking a language that you do not know? You hear it, but it sounds like noise. Lots of garbled sounds. Is it confusing? Overwhelming? What does the world of adult language sound like to an infant? Imagine how much has to happen for the typical child to grow to understand and use that language in just a few short years.

- less desirable behaviors:
  - pulling away
  - biting
  - kicking
  - pinching
  - throwing
  - grabbing
  - tantrums
  - self abuse
  - etc.

Functions of Communication:

In the beginning, the most common purposes or reasons (called *functions*) that children attempt to communicate with us are:

- pleasure: social attention, social interaction
- requesting: food, objects, to do something
- protesting: something I don't want, something I don't want to do, I am unhappy about something, I don't want to be near you, I don't want your attention

As they develop more social and communication maturity, children expand their reasons for communicating to include a wider variety of purposes *(functions)*, including:

- social greetings
- labeling pictures or objects or people
- asking questions
- answering questions
- commenting on something
- engaging in conversations for sharing thoughts and ideas
- expressing feelings such as boredom, fear, confusion, frustration, pain

Gee, you are talking about all kinds of skills I never thought about before. I can see how they are important. But what about speech? I still want to know about speech.

We are getting to the speech part! Remember that the development of all these communication skills is directly related to the maturation of the child's biological and neurological systems. As his cognitive skills increase, he is gradually able to do more things.

As the child continues to mature, numerous skills unfold. Consider these:

1. Children grow to recognize specific words that other people use. It comes from repetition. They hear those same words over and over related to a specific object or event and they begin to remember the connection. As a child's ability to remember develops, he will remember more and more words.

2. They gain more control and coordination over their own ability to make sounds and they begin to use sound to help them communicate their intents. Sounds are used for social interaction or to communicate their wants and needs.

3. They begin to imitate sounds, put sounds together and eventually create those same words that they hear other people use. Those first words are exciting because the child has finally figured out the relationship between the sounds he makes with his mouth and what he sees in the environment.

4. Children begin to recognize the power behind spoken communication. They recognize that spoken communication gives them the ability to communicate differently . . .to have control . . .and to "change the world."

Interwoven into this development are numerous skills that we call pragmatic skills. Pragmatic skills are like glue. They are all the invisible but related abilities that are necessary to create effective communication. The list of pragmatic skills can be long. It includes the preverbal skills such as effectively using gestures and participating in social turn-taking. Add establishing attention and staying involved in interactions. Effective conversation skills and repairing communication breakdowns are a few more on the list.

Think of pragmatic skills as the non-speech parts of communication. When they are there and working well, we don't even notice them. When there is a problem with them, we know something isn't right. It may take some analysis to figure out exactly what the problem is, but we know that something is odd or different or not functioning properly. Although many students with communication disorders can experience difficulty with pragmatic skills, those with autism spectrum disorders demonstrate the most severe difficulty in this area.

Pragmatic skills are those "invisible" skills that support communication to make it effective such as:

- *attending skills*
- *establishing eye contact*
- *conversation abilities*
- *appropriate use of gestures*
- *social turn-taking*
- *breakdown and repair skills*
- *and many other skills. . .*

The child's first words are exciting. It is a major accomplishment! Isn't that the goal?

It is exciting when we hear a word from a young child. First words are a milestone that stirs much attention. But they are just the first steps on a long journey. After those first words, children who are following a normal developmental path accomplish many other skills. Consider this information:

- Those first words that emerge at about one year of age multiply so rapidly that a five-year-old can comprehend and use a vocabulary of 10,000 to 15,000 words.

- After first words, children begin to put two words and short phrases together, eventually developing the ability to create complex sentences.

- Language has a whole grammar structure that children learn with little assistance.

- Children begin to learn the multiple meanings of words. (A *hot* stove will burn you. A *hot* car is a really fancy one.)

- They begin to put words together in creative ways. . . creating their own unique sentences to convey their own unique thoughts. They are not just reproducing exact patterns that they have been taught. They can invent sentences that they have never heard before.

- There is an increase in the child's ability to understand the abstract ideas and complex conversation of other people.

- Language eventually becomes a tool for conversation, humor, and understanding and sharing complex thoughts.

It is hard to imagine all the skills that need to develop from infancy to enable a child to eventually become a competent adult communicator. The point is, most of this complex process unfolds automatically. As long as a child is in an environment that provides proper interaction and stimulation, the child's internal circuits will guide the journey.

Why do some children have difficulty learning to talk? Why is learning communication hard for some children?

This is not an easy question to answer. The reasons may be different for each child. What we *do* know is that something is not working right in the child's biological and/or neurological system. Those skills that automatically emerge for other children do not develop the same way for these students. There could be many reasons why, and the context of this book will not be able to explore that. What will be helpful, however, is to explore what kinds of problems students have with communication. That knowledge will give us a foundation for seeing the relationship between communication and behavior. Once that is established, we will be able to use our understandings to provide support and teaching to begin solving the behavior problems that our students exhibit.

What are communication problems?

Communication and behavior are intertwined. Students are usually not "just being bad." Frequently, their communication machines don't run well. Understanding what can go wrong with their systems helps us more realistically define our expectations for them.

Even if a student speaks, he won't be an effective communicator if he demonstrates problems in pragmatic skills. Difficulty with social and pragmatic skills is most prevalent in autism spectrum disorders, although these problems frequently emerge as a part of many disabilities.

Considering how complicated the development of communication is, it is not surprising that some students encounter difficulties along the way. Students who experience mild disabilities may have a problem in one or two areas. Those students with more severe communication disorders will probably demonstrate difficulty in many of these areas. Identifying the *type* of problem a student is experiencing is a first step that leads to providing support and teaching. Here are some of the most common areas that students experience difficulty.

> *One of the primary characteristics of autism spectrum disorders is a disability in communication and social skills. It does not matter if a student is high skilled or low skilled. It does not matter if the student is verbal or non-verbal. By **definition**, these students experience difficulty in some aspect of communication and socialization. Frequently, the most challenging students are those who are verbal and higher skilled. On the surface they can appear to be more capable than they are, however, their difficulty with pragmatic skills can result in them appearing "different." The areas where they experience difficulty are more difficult to identify because they are subtle.*

Hearing or Vision Difficulties:

The senses of sound and sight are fundamental for developing communication skills. Just like in the general population, some children have *visual acuity* or *hearing acuity* problems. Hearing problems are suspected when we observe students who do not respond consistently to sound or the communication of others. Severe vision problems could also affect how a child responds in communication situations. When students cannot hear or see well, their communication ability will be affected. Sometimes obvious problems in these areas are not identified.

Another group of students can see and hear, however, they have a problem in some way with the sensory input. Either they do not understand what they see or hear, or they respond differently to the visual or auditory information.

Impaired Comprehension:

Students may experience significant difficulty *understanding* and *interpreting* communication and social information. They can hear and they can see, but their ability to establish meaning from the communication is affected.

They do not effectively understand what they hear. This can be caused by difficulty in establishing attention, how the brain processes the information and many other related functions. Sometimes these students are described as having auditory *processing problems*. These students may initially be evaluated because it is suspected that they do not hear. Once it is established that they *do* hear, the focus turns more toward determining how they understand what they hear.

Their difficulty can be in understanding the language and other communication forms a person is using. Even if they understand the words that are spoken, they may have a problem understanding and interpreting the ideas and concepts that are being communicated.

> **Example:** Susan doesn't respond when you verbally *tell* her what you want her to do. You have to point to what you want or physically prompt her to follow your directions.

> **Example:** Carlos tries to participate in conversations, however, he may give an answer to a different question than the question you are asking him.

*The difficulty that students with autism spectrum disorders have with **understanding** communication and social interaction is one of the most undiagnosed and most misunderstood aspects of this communication disorder.*

Example: If you tell Anthony to get something or give him directions how to do something, he may totally misinterpret what you want.

Example: Gene tries to have conversations with his classmates, but he does not seem to understand the questions that they ask him.

Example: Robin stopped eating cereal when she heard them talking about serial killers on the TV news.

Example: Hank was nagging his father about when they were going to the store. Hank is so literal in his understanding of language that when Dad said, "Hang on a minute!" he grabbed Dad's arm and held it tightly.

Ineffective Communicative Intent:

When the child uses some type of movement or vocalization with the purpose of getting the attention or response of another person, we call that *communicative intent.* He is doing something, on purpose, to convey some information to you or get a reaction from you. Some students demonstrate little or no communicative intent. Other students intend to communicate, however, the ways that they try are not effective. If they try in some way but don't get a response, they may give up trying. Another important part of communicative intent is persisting until the goal is accomplished. For communication to be effective, it is important for the student to recognize that he needs to send his message to another person and he needs to keep trying until there is a connection with that person.

Example: When Jennifer sees you eating her favorite gummy snacks she looks at those treats. When you keep eating gummy snacks, she keeps looking and hits herself on the head. No one realizes that looking and hitting herself are her ways of telling you she wants some.

Example: Laura is beginning to realize that a picture of a cookie can help her get a cookie. She walks over to a cookie picture hanging on the wall and points to it. Unfortunately, no one is there to receive her message. She doesn't understand that a person needs to be a part of her attempt to communicate.

Example: Timmy makes an unusual sound that Mom interprets to mean he wants to go to the bathroom. She takes him to the bathroom when he makes that sound. If Mom doesn't hear when Timmy makes the sound, he has an accident. He does not realize that he needs to get her attention or make his sound again.

Example: Jim talks a lot, but he always appears to be talking to himself. He doesn't understand how to use his speech to communicate information to other people.

Difficulty with Social Interaction:

The social skills of students with autism spectrum disorders can appear different from other students. Initiating social interactions or responding to the social intentions of other people, staying involved in social interactions, taking turns in communication exchanges, interpreting social situations, and accurately interpreting the communication of others are areas of difficulty.

Example: Stephanie walks up and hits people. It appears that this is a way of greeting them or trying to engage in social interaction. She needs to learn how to get attention in more appropriate ways.

Example: When you try to talk or play with Mark, he keeps running away to go jump up and down on the other side of the room. He needs to learn how to stay involved in an interaction.

Example: When Nathan was standing in line with the other students someone bumped him. Nathan responded as if he was being attacked. He did not understand that it was an accident.

Example: When students across the lunchroom were laughing and giggling, Shawn became upset because she thought they were laughing at her. She had a hard time understanding why they would be laughing.

Example: If a classmate approached and said "Hi", Brent would just ignore the student.

Example: Curtis is constantly looking at people's faces and asking, "Are you mad at me?"

Impaired Expression:

Normal communication involves both non-verbal and verbal *forms* of communication. Students may be limited in the variety of different forms of communication that they use. Students who do develop verbal skills may experience difficulties with the production of speech or with the structure or the content of their language.

Ineffective Non-Verbal Communication:

Some non-verbal students are very skilled at using gestures and other non-verbal forms of communication to get their wants and needs met. Even though they don't talk, they are very good communicators.

Our targeted students may have difficulty effectively using pointing to objects, gestures, body language, facial expressions and other means to help communicate their wants and needs. Whether they are verbal or not, they do not use these non-verbal skills well.

Example: When Jason wants something he cries. He doesn't seem to know how to tell you or show you what it is that he is crying about. You just have to guess.

Example: The expression on Lynne's face does not match the situation. She often has an angry look, even when you talk with her about something pleasurable.

Example: Josh laughs even when someone is angry with him.

Example: When Cindy is trying to tell you about something and she is having difficulty expressing herself, she keeps saying, "That, that." and she waves her arm in a direction. She needs to learn to point more effectively to help communicate her message.

Speech Problems:

Some students are unable to produce words or use their voices effectively for communication purposes. Three common problems are:

Difficulty producing voice, speech sounds or words *on request* or *on purpose.* Occasionally he can do it, but not consistently. Perhaps he can vocalize spontaneously. . . .almost by accident like when he is playing. Perhaps he can say some words automatically to request or protest, but he can't do the same thing again on purpose or when you want him to.

> **Example:** Timothy is a very silent child. He rarely makes sounds or vocal noises. When he does vocalize, he doesn't make many different sounds. He usually cannot imitate your speech sounds if you try to get him to do that.

> **Example:** Alexis usually cannot say words when you try to get her to talk, but when she gets mad, whole sentences come out of her mouth.

> **Example:** Sometimes Arthur can say a word to make a request and sometimes he can't. It is very inconsistent. But he can say "no" quite easily.

Producing speech only for certain purposes. Perhaps students can sing songs, recite the alphabet, count, or repeat phrases from TV and videos. Frequently the vocalizations they can produce are set to music or are rhythmic and repetitive. The student may use these vocalizations for participation with another person or with a video or tape. Sometimes these vocalizations are produced for self-enjoyment or self-stimulation. They are generally not used for intentional communication to get a want or need met. He probably does not use the vocalizations for communication purposes and he may not be able to vocalize those words or other vocabulary on request.

> **Example:** Jeff counts and sings the alphabet song. In fact, he can recite every word from his favorite video. If you try to get him to say or repeat different words, he usually can't do it.

> **Example:** Allison doesn't use any words to communicate, but if you listen closely you can hear her sing along with her favorite song on her favorite video.

Difficulty speaking clearly. The student is unable to smoothly coordinate the movements of the tongue, lips and other structures of the mouth, which results in poor articulation or unclear speech. When the student tries to say words, they do not come out very clear.

> **Example:** Colleen tries to tell you what she wants, but the words are not intelligible. She does not put many of the sounds in them and it is very hard to figure out what she is saying.

> **Example:** When Harry tries to say words they all come out as one-syllable words. His speech sounds like grunts and garbled sounds, mostly vowels.

Language Delay or Disorder:

As students learn language they may not have learned enough words to communicate what they really want to say. Sometimes students have learned words but they cannot always find the right words to use when they want to use them. Common language problems include:

The student has very few words that he knows how to use. Because he has just a few, he may try to use them over and over for many different purposes.

> **Example:** Roger uses three words: "cookie", "potty", and "no". Anytime he wants something to eat, he says cookie, regardless what the choices are. He says "no" frequently. He seems to use "no" as a way of responding to a request rather than actually protesting something.

They cannot easily find the specific words to use when they are trying to express themselves. Some students seem to know a greater number of words. Sometimes they try, but they retrieve the wrong words. The words the student ends up using do not really communicate the message he is attempting to share.

> **Example:** Justin takes Mom by the hand and pulls her to the kitchen. He says "cookie." When Mom hands him the cookie he cries and screams and says "cookie" again. Mom hands him a cookie again. After he continues to cry, out of desperation, Mom hands him some juice and he is happy.

It is estimated that 50% of students with autism spectrum disorders are non-verbal or have very limited verbal skills. That percentage is a fluctuating number. The continued increase in identifying students who are higher skilled or have a milder disability is bound to affect the numbers. Other special needs populations have some non-verbal students. The more severely cognitively disabled populations have a greater percentage of students who do not learn to talk.

Sometimes students have to *think* for what seems like a *very* long time to try to retrieve the right word. Perhaps they can find the words more easily when they are speaking spontaneously, but they have a harder time finding them when they are under pressure to give an answer. The more stress they are under, the harder it is for them to produce the language. It may take them a very long time to respond because they are searching for the right answer. Looking at pictures of objects may help them recall the proper words more easily.

> **Example:** When you ask Carolyn a question she sits there and smiles very nicely but it takes her forever to give you an answer.

> **Example:** When you ask Michelle which book she wants to read she thinks hard and can't come up with an answer. If you show her some choices, she can answer quite quickly.

They seem to talk a lot without saying very much. Some students have the ability to use more language, however, they do not have the ability to communicate ideas very clearly.

> **Example:** Michael talks a lot. He never stops talking. When you try to have a conversation with him, he talks but does not seem to really say anything. Even though he uses a lot of words he does not really answer a question. He needs to learn to use fewer words that express a specific idea.

> **Example:** David blurts out answers to questions very quickly. The problem is he doesn't take time to think and the answer he gives might not have anything to do with the question, even if you know that he knows the correct answer. He needs to learn to wait and think before answering so he can have more control over the words he is using.

> **Example:** Jerry is very social. He loves to monopolize the conversation. The flow of his speech sounds good at first. Then you realize that when he talks he seems to fill in with non-words or made up words (jargon). Consequently, the real message he is attempting to communicate is not clear.

Other Language and Communication Differences:

Unusual Speaking Style: Some students talk in an unusual style such as in a monotone or with robot-like or sing-song-like speech.

> **Example:** Cynthia gets teased because the other students say she talks like a robot.

Echolalia: Some students repeat or echo the language that they hear. *Immediate echolalia* is repeating the words that the other person is saying to them rather than answering a question or using their own language to respond.

> **Example:** Whenever someone asks Malcolm a question, he repeats the question. If the teacher says, "Malcolm, where are your glasses?", Malcolm responds, "Where are your glasses?"

Delayed echolalia is when the student repeats memorized words or phrases that he had heard before. It can be language that someone else has used or it may be language they have heard from another source like the TV. Students may try to tell you something by using these memorized phrases instead of trying to create their own sentences. Sometimes they repeat the echo language but they are not intending to communicate to anyone.

> **Example:** Todd greets people by walking up and singing, "You deserve a break today!"

Perseveration: When students don't have the ability to use a wide variety of language, they may try to communicate what is important to them by repeating the same things over and over again. That constant repetition is called perseveration.

> **Example:** Jonathan is going to the circus on Thursday. He is so excited that he can hardly contain himself. He asks, "Go to circus Thursday?" about five million times a day. He really seems to want to talk about the circus, but he doesn't know what else to say.

> **Example:** Marty is enthralled with PowerWarriors. He says, "Shazaam, PowerWarrior Man!" about twelve thousand times a day. Sometimes he says it to himself and sometimes he says it when he is attempting to engage in a conversation with someone else.

Using echolalic language is not necessarily a bad thing. It is a style of learning to communicate. An educational goal to eliminate echolalia may not produce desirable results. Instead, a goal to "increase the number of things the students can say" will help the student become a more effective communicator.

Ineffective Conversation Skills: Just like there is a difference between walking and dancing, conversation skills are different from just talking. Having a conversation with someone requires being able to take turns and make judgements about a constantly changing set of circumstances. Common areas of difficulty include:

- how to start a conversation
- responding when someone else starts a conversation
- staying involved in the conversation
- taking turns in the conversation
- developing a topic of conversation
- staying on the topic of the conversation
- knowing how and when to terminate the conversation

Example: Kevin walks up to other students and says something to them that he knows makes them mad so he will get a reaction from them. When they get mad, he laughs. He doesn't seem to have more appropriate ways to socialize with them.

Example: Tyrone walks up to zillions of people each day asking, "What color is your police car?" He wants to socialize, however, he doesn't know other ways to begin a conversation.

Example: Brad has a fixation for basketball. Whenever someone tries to engage him in conversation he takes his turn by mentioning some basketball information. He frequently interjects, "He shoots. . .he scores!" in his conversations. Whatever the topic, Brad brings it back to basketball. He needs to be able to talk about some other topics.

Example: When Sara tries to have a conversation she keeps talking and talking and talking. She never stops. Finally the other people just go away. Sara needs to learn to take turns with a conversation partner.

Recognizing and Repairing Communication Breakdowns: When students are attempting to communicate to you they may not realize when you do not understand. If they do realize that you don't understand, they may not know what else to do to get their message across. If they do not understand when you are communicating to them, they may not know how to tell you they don't understand.

> **Example:** Jack tries to tell people what he wants but no one can understand his speech attempts. When no one understands, he has a tantrum. Jack needs to learn how to point or show an object or use some other way to get his message across.

> **Example:** If you tell Elisa to do something and she doesn't understand, she just stands there and looks at you. She doesn't know how to let you know she doesn't understand.

How do communication problems affect behavior?

Well, now I am overwhelmed. There are so many ways students can have communication problems. How do these problems affect behavior?

Behavior and communication are intertwined. It is critical to remember that these students communicate *differently*. What they understand and how they attempt to communicate to others may not be what is typical for their peers. We have explored just a sampling of the types of problems they can have. This is what you need to remember. Behavior situations frequently occur because:

1. The students don't understand

- Students have difficulty understanding the social cues and clues in their environment.

- They experience problems understanding and interpreting the communication of others.

- They don't participate effectively because they don't understand what they need to learn.

- Behavior problems result from the student's misunderstandings and confusions.

- Behavior problems occur because other people don't understand that the students don't understand.

Communication breakdown describes those instances when the communication message does not work. Someone is attempting to communicate a message but the communication partner does not understand. The most critical skill is to **recognize** when there is a communication breakdown. Then, if the message is not getting across, does the person who is attempting to communicate realize that the message is not being understood? If the message is not understood, does the person attempt to use another form of communication to try to repair the breakdown? First you have to recognize that there is a breakdown. Then it is necessary to do something to **repair** the breakdown. Many students with communication challenges do not know how to do this. Many adult communication partners are also lacking in this skill.

> Sometimes when people are very focused on a child learning to talk, they **expect** speech, **demand** speech or **accept** only speech. They do not respond to all the other communication forms a student attempts to use. Even if the non-verbal communication strategies the student is using are communicating clearly, they are not recognized for their value. Caution is needed. It is important to remember that **all** forms of communication have value. An effective communication system contains **many forms**, not just speech.

> **When we expect a form of communication that is too difficult for a student, he may either withdraw from interacting with you or he may resort to using behaviors that make his point more emphatically.**

2. The students have difficulty expressing themselves

- People don't realize the students are attempting to communicate.

- In some instances, the communication partner expects a different *form* of communication and does not respond to what the student is attempting to communicate.

- People don't interpret the student's speech, communication attempts or behavior accurately.

- The student's communication attempts do not adequately communicate his wants and needs.

- The student uses behavior to try to accomplish his goals because that works better for him than the other forms of communication he knows how to use.

3. The students don't know what else to do

- Students do what they know how to do.

- They need to learn new or different skills to help them participate in their life routines more effectively.

THE POINT IS: Communication is more than just speech. It is a complex process that requires the interconnection of many different skills. Even if students appear to be developing communication skills, it is important to remember that their communication systems may not work efficiently or effectively.

- They have acquired a limited number of communication skills.

- The skills that they have do not work very well to help them understand their environment or get their wants and needs met.

- Difficulty with communication skills is a major cause of behavior problems.

REMEMBER: Students will use what works best for them.

- If they don't understand what to do, they will do what they think they are supposed to do.

- If they attempt to communicate their wants and needs and people don't understand, they may try another way . . . perhaps using a behavior that is less desirable (from our point of view) but works better (from their point of view).

- When they get frustrated, they *will* let you know.

If communication is such a significant problem for these students, what is the remedy?

It would be nice to think there is something we can do to "fix" the students so they won't have any more communication difficulties or behavior problems. Unfortunately, that is not a realistic goal. But, there are two things we can do that will *significantly* impact the lives of these students.

> • Improve Understanding
> • Teach Skills

The goal is to help the student develop a *variety* of skills -*a whole system*- that will help him:

- get his wants and needs met more effectively

- interact with other people in a manner that is mutually enjoyable

- participate effectively in his life activities and routines

- increase understanding

In order to successfully accomplish these goals it is necessary to identify a student's *learning strengths*.

Problems! We keep talking about problems. Do these students have strengths? What are their strengths? Is this where visual strategies fits in?

Bingo! A very large percentage of students with autism and other moderate to severe communication handicaps are *visual learners*. That means they understand what they *see* better than what they *hear*. As we discuss this further, it will become obvious why using visual strategies is a highly effective way to improve communication and successfully modify their behavior problems.

Chapter 3

What Are Visual Strategies?

Do you consider yourself an auditory learner or a visual learner? When this author asks that question to audiences, about 95% of the people put themselves in the visual learner category. Perhaps our students with communication disorders are not that different from us. Why are they affected more? We are probably better at compensating when we experience difficulty.

*It is important to remember that visual communication is the **most effective** communication **form** for most students.*

Recognizing that people have different learning styles leads to the discovery that most students with autism spectrum disorders and many others with moderate to severe communication disabilities are *visual learners*. That means they understand what they *see* better than they understand what they *hear*. The significance of this observation has immeasurable implications for communication, social interactions, and learning. An inability to effectively take in and process auditory information can be a *significant* factor affecting the student's appropriate behavior and participation.

If these students are visual learners, what do we need to do?

We need to communicate more visually. These students live and learn in environments that are highly verbal. Think about how we communicate with each other. We talk. And we talk. And we talk some more.

While it is common for educational programming to focus on teaching communication skills, that focus in most settings tends to be directed primarily toward developing the student's *expressive* communication skills; helping them express their wants and needs. Comparatively little attention is aimed toward increasing the student's ability to *understand* the communication in his life.

How do we help them understand better?

Use visual tools and supports to provide the structure and routine that are so critical to the lives of these students. Visual tools are used to:
- give students information
- give directions
- teach social skills
- organize their environment
- establish rules and behavior guidelines
- teach academic skills and work tasks
- support learning expressive communication skills
- and many more ways to make communication more effective

What are visual tools and supports?

Things you can *see*. Think about the forms of communication that we use that you can see.

1. First, think about yourself as a visual tool. Observe how you can support communication with gestures and body movements such as:
- smiling or frowning
- shaking and nodding your head
- holding out your hand
- holding up an object
- pointing
- and lots more

2. Then think about the things that occur naturally in the environment that we can use as visual tools to help students understand.
- objects, people
- pictures, posters, photographs
- printed material, books, labels, signs
- anything you see

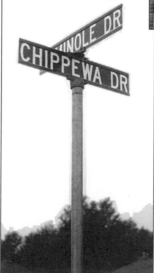

3. If we need more visual tools, we can create them. We can specially design visual tools to meet specific needs the students have.
  * schedules
  * calendars
  * choice boards
  * rule charts
  * lists
  * printed instructions
  * behavior reminders
  * lots of tools to help students understand and know what to do

What do the visual tools and supports do? Why do we use them?

Visual tools and supports provide the structure that helps students participate effectively and avoid many behavior difficulties. In the midst of their difficulties, capitalizing on their visual strength results in the use of visual strategies to teach skills and to support communication. This approach has provided the structure necessary to substantially alter many difficult behavior situations. If behavior problems do erupt, visual tools provide a means to help the student modify his behavior. Primary reasons for using visual tools and supports are:
  * Improve communication – both understanding and expression
  * Give students information
  * Support the student through his life routines
  * Teach skills
  * Prevent problems
  * Intervene when there is a problem

What do you accomplish by using visual tools and supports? What is your goal?

There are lots, but some of the most important goals are:
- Get student attention
- Improve understanding
- Decrease fear and anxiety
- Support appropriate behavior and participation
- Improve expressive communication
- Teach self-regulation so students learn to manage their own behavior
- Teach self-management for independence
- Increase success of the student across settings and situations

Visual tools and supports become a major form of communication for the interaction and learning in the student's life.

How does this relate to behavior?

There are many reasons that behavior problems occur. As you search for the causes of the problems, it becomes obvious that difficulty with communication is interwoven. When you pursue the solutions, communication emerges as a need.

◄••►

THE REAL BOTTOM LINE IS THIS:

Students with autism spectrum disorders and others who experience moderate to severe communication disorders frequently have behavior difficulties because they don't understand their world very well and they are not effective in getting their wants and needs met. *They tend to be visual learners living in a very auditory world.* Because they are easily frustrated and often misunderstood, their behavior is frequently not like that of other students. Sometimes they do not understand how to do what other students do. Sometimes they try to control the world using behaviors and strategies other students don't usually need to use. The result is a frustrated student. He is taught by parents and teachers who are frequently discouraged and anxious and sometimes baffled by what he does or does not do.

In attempting to sort out the challenges, we discover a comparative learning strength. These students tend to understand what they *see* better than what they *hear*. Simple logic says teach to their strength. Use that strength to compensate for their weaknesses. Hence visual strategies.

◄••►

Most important: Using visual strategies works! These techniques work for verbal students. They work for non-verbal students. High or low skilled students both benefit from visual supports that are designed to match their level of capability. Visual tools and supports are not a magic Band-Aid that will fix every problem that these students have, but they will provide a valuable framework to support their lives. Using visual tools and supports makes a difference. A huge difference. That is what the rest of this book is about. Lots of ideas. Lots of suggestions about how to do it.*

---

*Editor's note: The book *Visual Strategies for Improving Communication* gives a more in-depth explanation of the how and why. It is full of samples and examples and lots of how-to information.

Part 2

ASSESSMENT CONSIDERATIONS

Chapter 4

Evaluating Behavior Situations

The most important part of dealing with behavior situations is the evaluation or assessment of the problem. Without a thorough assessment of the student and his behavior difficulties, behavior management becomes a series of *reactions* to specific actions or events *rather than a plan* for supporting long term improvement.

It is very common for people to react in some way to the student's behavior without assessing the *cause* of the behavior. When the student does a specific behavior, they determine a specific consequence to intervene and stop the behavior. Unfortunately, this approach frequently produces more frustrations than it solves problems. *Unless the cause of the behavior is addressed in some way, the behavior is likely to keep recurring.* For example:

- Jenny keeps taking off her shoes. The consequence is that she has to sit in the square until she puts her shoes back on. If no one figures out that she is taking off her shoes because something hurts her foot, they will have a power struggle with Jenny all day.

- David grabs food from the student sitting next to him. The consequence is that David is removed from the table for one minute. Unfortunately, this consequence does not teach David how to make an appropriate request so he won't grab food anymore.

A thorough assessment will guide us to the answers that we need to solve the behavior problems our students demonstrate.

What kind of test do you recommend using to assess behavior problems? I want to buy one!

The most critical tool for successful assessment is the power of *observation*. Skillful observation is like watching a movie. In the movie theatre you watch the star of the show, but you also pay attention to all the supporting cast, the scenery, the music, and the other elements that create the story. Assessing behavior requires that same alertness to detail. You follow what the student is doing, but you also pay attention to all the other contributing parts.

1. We need to view a problem behavior in the context of the student's immediate environment.

2. Next, it is critical to target the *cause of the behavior.*

3. Then we need to balance that information with our understanding of the student's capabilities and special needs.

4. The combination of information provides the direction to a viable solution.

Assessment occurs as we observe how the student handles himself in situations, locations, or interactions that result in difficulty. The better we can see the problem behavior in the context of a "big picture", the more efficiently we will be able to plan solutions.

TOOLS FOR ASSESSMENT

There are various assessment methods and testing procedures that are used for behavior observation.

ABC

One popular recording format is called **ABC**. This is a simple way to collect information to help you think about what is happening and to look at the behavior in the context of a whole event, not just a specific action. The goal is to record:

- The **Antecedent** (what happens before the behavior problem occurs)

- The **Behavior** (what the student does)

- The **Consequence** (what happens after. . . . what the result of the behavior is)

BEHAVIOR OBSERVATION		
Antecedent	Behavior	Consequence

The ABC approach is an easy way to look logically at the "big picture." It guides us to view behavior in a way that helps determine what causes it.

Functional Behavior Analysis

There are various systems people use to analyze the behaviors that students exhibit. Analyzing those behaviors to determine their *purposes* or *functions* is called a functional behavior analysis. The goal of a functional behavior analysis is to *systematically* look at all the information necessary to develop a plan for long-term change. Writing down the information you collect can help the analysis of the situation.

Data Collection

Another simple tool to guide our observations is to take data. There are many ways data can help us with problem solving. The most common uses are to:

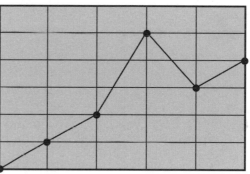

- Record when a problem occurs during the student's life routines

- Determine specifically what the student does or does not do

- Keep track of how many times a student does or does not do something – how frequently a problem occurs

- Confirm change in the student's behavior or performance

Data collection helps confirm our memory for events. When we change something or do something different, data helps us know if that change results in a real difference in the student's behavior.

How do you know what to do to solve the problems? That is what I really want to know!

There is no magic formula. The Guide for Assessing Behavior Situations will help. The tool is designed to guide your observation and thinking about the behaviors you are dealing with. Because each child is different and each problem behavior is unique, the answers need to unfold.

ABC, functional behavior analysis and data collection give us some ways to gather information about what is occurring. They help us begin to discover *what the problem is,* but those tools do not give us any *answers* about what do after we figure out what the problem is. The *Guide for Assessing Behavior Situations* will lead you to some solutions. It will aim toward strategies discussed in this book. This tool is not intended to replace other evaluation or observation tools, but to supplement other assessment approaches. This assessment tool will not solve all your problems, but it will provide a framework for evaluating and better understanding many of them.

ASSESSING BEHAVIOR SITUATIONS

What is the Guide for Assessing Behavior Situations?

This tool has five parts. The material discussed in this book will help you answer the questions. While you are pondering the answers, think about these points.

Describing the Situation: (See Chapter 1 for more in-depth discussion)

An effective assessment of a behavior situation requires some initial information.

- First, we need to know some specific details about who the student is. All behavior problems need to be viewed in relationship to the student's age and skill level. One of the most important pieces of information we need is an estimate of his ability level or functioning level. This *does not* mean an actual IQ score. It *does* mean we need to determine if a student is functioning at age level, moderately below age level or at a severely impaired level. This information will guide us to realistic expectations for the student. What is expected at one skill level is not appropriate for another skill level. It is surprising how many people claim they don't know what a student's functioning level is. Without this information we risk having expectations that the student will never be able to achieve.

- Assessment begins with an objective, thorough description of the problem. This needs to occur before adequate solutions can be identified. Don't skip this step!

- If the behavior exists, it is already being responded to in some way. Is there anything being done to prevent the behavior from occurring? How does the student respond to the prevention techniques currently used? Does the current system work or not work? Why? How do others respond to the behavior? What is the result?

- Putting the problem behavior in perspective will help us choose what to deal with. It is impossible to try to change everything a student does. Pick the most important things to teach.

Analyzing and Interpreting the Behavior: (See Chapters 1&2 for more in-depth discussion)

Once we describe the behavior, we need to attempt to interpret what we see. We need to analyze the information to help us make sense of what we are observing. That helps us understand *why* the behavior occurs. This step is essential before finding effective, long-term solutions.

- Behavior problems are rarely simple events. The better we understand the situation from the student's point of view, the more effective our solutions will be.

- The communication partner or the person directly involved in a behavior situation may have a very different perspective from the student.

- An outside observer may view a situation differently from those people directly involved. It is often easier to see the whole picture when you are not actively involved in an interaction.

- Sometimes the cause and the purpose of a behavior will be evident. There will be times when the answers are not clear. In those situations it may become necessary to guess or hypothesize until you can get more information. When you use your hypothesis to plan a remedy, it will become evident if you were right. If the student responds to your solution, you were probably right.

Developing Solutions: (See Chapters 1&2 for more in-depth discussion)

- The first goal is to prevent problems from occurring. That is ideal, but not always possible.

- The second goal is to have the tools to handle a problem when it does occur.

- Remember that *taking no action* can be just as important as taking action, depending on the circumstances.

Choosing Strategies: (See Chapter 3 for more in-depth discussion-then the rest of this book will outline a variety of options)

- Since communication is frequently part of the problem, communication generally needs to evolve as a part of the solution.

- Since visual strategies are an important part of an effective communication system, they need to be a strong consideration for any plan to change behavior.

- Sometimes the most important changes are those made by the communication partner. How the communication partner modifies his communication or actions can significantly affect the student's behavior.

Evaluating the New Plan:

Ongoing evaluation tells us if what we are doing is creating the results we want. Evaluation and observation are an essential part of behavior management.

Use the *Guide for Assessing Behavior Situations* to help you discover simple but effective solutions to behavior problems.

Guide for Assessing Behavior Situations

Who is the student?

Name: _____

Age: _____

Diagnosis: _____

Overall Ability Level/Functioning Level: _____

Communication Skills: _____

    Understanding: _____

    Expression: _____

Social Skill Ability: _____

Other Observations: _____

Special Considerations: _____

Describe the Behavior Problem

The Behavior Itself

What specifically does the student do?

What specifically does the student fail to do?

QuirkRoberts PUBLISHING

The Circumstances

What else is happening when the behavior occurs?

When do problems occur?

- What time of day?

- During what activities?

Where does the problem occur?

- Any specific locations?

How frequently does behavior occur?

- Is there a pattern?

The Aftermath

What does the student do after the behavior occurs?

How is the behavior currently handled?

- Is anything being done to prevent the behavior from occurring?

- How does the student respond to the current prevention techniques?

- How is the behavior managed or responded to when it does occur?

- Does the current management system work?

The Significance

Why should this behavior be addressed?

- Annoying habit

- Things I want changed

- Really annoying behavior

- Behaviors that cause problems

- Behaviors causing really major problems

- Behaviors I can't stand any more

- Behaviors preventing life routines

- Behaviors preventing learning

- Behaviors causing injury

The Desired Situation

What should the student do?

What should the student stop doing?

What change is desired?

Other observations:

QuirkRoberts PUBLISHING

From the <u>Student's</u> Perspective

Does the student have a problem?

○ Bothered by something

○ Wants something he can't have

○ Does not feel good

○ Doesn't know how to do something

○ Doesn't want something

○ No problem - just doing what comes naturally

○ Other

○ Cannot tolerate specific people or situations

○ Specific reactions to people or situations

○ Does something inappropriate

○ Cannot repair the communication breakdown

○ Doesn't know what to do

What does the function (purpose) of the communication or behavior appear to be?

Is there communicative intent?

    ○ Seek social interaction
    ○ Get attention
    ○ Avoid social interaction

    ○ Request
    ○ Protest

    ○ Gain information
    ○ Give information

    ○ Escape

    ○ Conversation

    ○ Other

Does the behavior appear to be *non*-interactive?

    ○ Self-stimulation

    ○ Other:

What does the student *want* to happen?

What does the student *expect* to happen?

Does the behavior accomplish the student's goal?

QUIRK ROBERTS PUBLISHING

From the <u>Communication Partner's</u> Perspective

Is there a communication breakdown?

What is the nature of the breakdown?

    The Student:

        ○ Doesn't understand

        ○ Can't express self

        ○ Other

    The Communication Partner:

        ○ Doesn't understand student

        ○ Must communicate to student differently

        ○ Other

QUIRKROBERTS
PUBLISHING

From the <u>Observer's/Analyzer's</u> Perspective

What might be the cause of the behavior?

○ Appropriate for student's age

○ Appropriate for the developmental level

○ Social skill problem

○ Communication breakdown

○ Learning style difference

○ Childish behavior

○ Sensory issue

○ Environment

○ Medical need

○ Family issue

○ Learned behavior

○ Other

Is there one cause?

More than one cause?

All of the above!

Developing Solutions

What must happen to solve the problem?

Alter what is causing the behavior
and / or
Change the adult's response to the problem behavior
and / or
Replace the problem behavior with a more acceptable behavior

AIM FOR PREVENTION

(before problem begins)

- ○ Identify causes
- ○ Teach skills
- ○ Offer alternatives

AIM FOR INTERVENTION

(after problem occurs)

- ○ Identify causes
- ○ Teach skills
- ○ Offer alternatives

Visual strategies can become an integral part of both prevention and intervention.

What must be done to change the problem behavior?

Support Communication

- ○ Improve understanding
- ○ Improve expression

Teach

- ○ Teach a new skill
- ○ Develop a routine

Modify Environment

- ○ Physical environment – the surroundings
- ○ Functional environment – the activities
- ○ Other people

Get Medical Attention

Accommodate for Sensory Need

TAKE NO ACTION

- ○ Live with it because it won't change
- ○ Wait until child outgrows it
- ○ Ignore it and it will go away

QuirkRoberts PUBLISHING

Choosing Strategies

Where does communication fit in?

○ Improve understanding

○ Improve expression

○ Increase social skills

○ Increase social understanding

○ Learn specific skills

○ Organize life

○ Regulate own behavior

○ Self-management

○ Other:

Consider Visual Strategies:

○ To support understanding

○ To organize the environment

○ To make requests and choices

○ To support self-management

○ To give information

○ To teach skills

○ To teach specific communication skills

○ To give directions

○ To support expression

○ To teach behavior regulation

○ Other:

How could visual strategies become part of the solution? How would they be used?

○ To alter the cause

○ To teach a different skill

○ To change the way the behavior is responded to

○ Teach the student a different response

○ Other

QUIRKROBERTS
PUBLISHING

Creating Change

What does the <u>communication partner</u> need to do?

○ Modify communication style

○ Modify teaching style

○ Change something that causes the problem

○ Change how the problem is responded to

○ Alter environment

○ Teach the student a skill

○ Other:

Implementing a Plan

What visual tools or strategies already exist?

○ How should they be used?

○ What changes should be made?

What visual tools or strategies need to be developed?

○ What will visual tools look like?

○ Where will they be located?

○ Who will use them?

○ When will they be used?

○ How will they be used?

What procedures will be followed to support students to prevent or eliminate opportunities for behavior challenges?

What procedures will be employed to teach appropriate skills?

What procedures will be established to intervene or change situations when problems arise?

QuirkRoberts PUBLISHING

Evaluating the New Plan

What happened?

Did something change?

Did the changes result in changes in the student's behavior?

How did the student's behavior change?

Did the changes result in satisfactory behavior?

What is the next step?

Keep doing what is being done because it works.

Add more strategies to help solve this problem.

Modify what is being done because what has been done so far is not working.

Address a different problem or situation.

Part 3

IMPROVING COMMUNICATION

Behavior problems, communication and visual strategies intertwine closely. Since communication breakdowns are an integral part of many behavior difficulties, improving communication is a prime goal. This chapter will highlight some significant skills to improve communication in both the student and in his communication partners. These skills are foundations for effective communication interactions.

The critical skills students need are foundation stones that the rest of communication is built upon. These are significantly important for visual strategies to really make a difference. They will support the use of visual tools and using visual tools will enhance the development of these skills.

Communication partners need to remember that they are an important part of the student's success. People are visual tools. The way they handle themselves can make the difference between behavior problems and communication success.

Once these foundation skills are in place, using visual tools and supports will achieve the maximum potential.

5

C h a p t e r

Ten Keys To Becoming A Better Communication Partner

Developing effective communication interaction skills is a critical need for students with autism spectrum disorders and those with other communication disabilities.

I have some students who are very difficult to communicate with. No matter how hard I try, I often feel like I am not connecting with them.

It is easy to think of what skills we want the *students* to learn. It can be a *greater* challenge to observe *our own* communication style and then modify our techniques as necessary to really connect with them. Little things that *we* do can help *us* become better "communication partners" with our students. This is especially important when working with students who are difficult to interact with. These keys will enhance your success.

1. Get on the student's level

Think about how frequently students are towered over by adults. Commonly, students are physically smaller than the adults are or they are sitting while adults are standing or other combinations that create great distances between faces.

- Sit, bend, squat or whatever you need to do to get your face at the child's eye level. You may need to move your body or the child's body to make this happen.

2. Establish attention

You have to become more interesting than whatever else is in the environment.

- Get physically close to the child. Some children do not respond well until you are just a few inches or a few feet away from them. Trying to connect from across the room doesn't do it. Be aware, however, that some students react negatively when people get too close to them. Careful observation will help you determine an effective distance.

- Get yourself in the child's line of vision. If the child turns his head it is natural to want to turn him back to face you. It may actually work better to move your own body to place yourself into his visual field.

- Watch for the student to *orient* to you. It is not necessary for a student to stare you down with eye contact. Turning his body or face in your direction or shifting his eye gaze may be enough to demonstrate he is paying attention.

- Become animated. As animated as you need to be. This can mean feeling a bit silly. Exaggerated facial expressions, gestures or body movements can help. Also try changing the volume, speed, and intonation of your voice.

- Use visual props. Hold an object or a picture of what you are talking about. Hold that prop in the child's visual field. Move it around until you are sure he sees it. Try holding the prop in front of you or near your face or mouth so he can see both.

> Some people with autism spectrum disorders have stated that they can **look** or they can **listen**, but it is difficult for them to do both at the same time. Perhaps this is a part of the reason for their poor eye contact.

3. Prepare the student for what you are going to communicate

It can take a moment for students to shift their attention to you. Many times these students demonstrate a slight delay in this skill. If you begin to communicate too quickly, they may miss important information.

Use a verbal signal to cue the student to get ready to receive your message. Try saying the student's name or a preparatory utterance such as:

- "look"
- "listen"
- "watch"
- "oh oh"
- "OK"
- "ready"

- Pair a verbal signal with a gesture when you are unsure if you have the student's attention.

- Use a visual prop to help him shift his thinking to the topic you are going to talk about. This is particularly helpful when you are shifting from one topic or activity to another.

4. Use gestures and body language meaningfully

Gestures and body language are very important for clarifying communication. They help a student pay attention and understand what you are saying. *How* they are used can make a huge difference in their effectiveness. Just waving your hands around while you are talking will not improve communication. Fast flitting movements that are not directly related to your communication can actually detract from the message you are trying to convey. *Purposeful* movements can enhance your interactions.

- Exaggerate movements. Making movements larger than normal helps attract attention.

- Use gestures and body movements in a slow, pronounced way. Pause for a dramatic effect. When shaking your head, extend the length of time you shake it. When making a facial grimace, hold that expression for an extended time.

- If you are pointing, hold that point long enough. Hold the position. Students may not easily attend to a tapping, moving point. Remember that a good point can be invaluable in helping the student orient to a *mutual referent.* When you are both looking at the same thing, communication effectiveness increases.

- Remember that communication is not just speech. Your hands, face, and body are critically important communication tools.

*A **mutual referent** is something that both people are paying attention to at the same time.*

5. Support your communication *visually*

Visual supports accomplish many purposes. Ultimately, they help the student participate more effectively. When you, as a communication partner, assume the responsibility for using some visual supports, you greatly improve your interaction with the student. This makes your social exchanges more enjoyable for both.

• Remember that visual supports are not just pictures. Pictures are wonderful, however, they are only one *form* of visual tool. Your body is a visual tool. Objects, people, TV guides, written messages, calendars and anything else you see can be a visual tool.

6. Speak slowly and clearly

If you have ever listened to the kinds of messages that people leave on answering machines, you realize the average person does not always communicate clearly. Mumbling, stumbling, starting over, forgetting and interjecting non-sequential information are common. Sometimes people start one sentence, start a second sentence, and then finish the first sentence. Students with communication difficulties cannot follow this clutter. In addition, students with communication challenges frequently process language more slowly than we do. If we speak quickly, our speech can sound like fast forward on the tape recorder. Those of us who are "non-stop-talkers" make it especially difficult for students. Slowing down can improve communication significantly. Talk so slow that it even feels funny. Then you will probably be talking at the right speed.

7. Limit verbalization

More talk is *not* better. Many of us were trained in a teaching model that suggested talking more would help students understand better. That is not true. Talking *less* is what helps, particularly for those of us who tend to be real talkers. One-word utterances and short phrases can frequently be more effective than long, extended sentences. One way to help judge how much language to use is to match the student's verbal output. If a student speaks in short phrases, he will understand one-word utterances and short phrases better than longer sentences.

How to use visual supports: It is frequently helpful to present the visual tool to the student first. That helps establish his attention. Then, when he is paying attention, you can give a simple verbal direction or comment. If you speak too soon, you may be done talking before he has time to shift his attention to you.

"I'm confused with this part. How is talking less good for people who like to talk???" Because these students are not capable of understanding the quantity of speech we use. **They cannot listen at the speed that we talk.** *When we slow down and use less language, they can take in the information better. Think of filling an empty pop bottle with water. If the water is turned on full blast there is too much water to go through the opening easily. It pours down the sides of the bottle. If the water is turned down, it can go into the opening more easily without spilling.*

8. Include "wait time" in your interactions

When you ask a question, wait for a moment before expecting a response. When giving a direction, pause for a moment to give the student time to process the request. Many of these students experience some delay in the amount of time it takes for their brains to process what is requested and then to figure out how to respond. It is a bit like when you turn the computer on. You need to wait for it to "boot up" before typing. It is easy for adults to jump in and make the request again or give the student help without waiting to give him the time he needs to respond.

- Count to five or ten or twenty (to yourself) when you ask a question or make a request. Observe how long it takes the student to respond. Don't be surprised if five or ten seconds feels like an eternity. It will when you are waiting.

- Wait *expectantly*. That means *look* at the student and look for his response as if you are waiting. The minute you become distracted by other things, you have diminished your opportunity.

- *Stay engaged* with the child while you are waiting. Sustain your eye contact. Do what you need to do to keep the child attending to you during this waiting time. For some children this can be very difficult. It may be necessary to move something for the student to stay engaged. You might have to move your body to get back into his visual field. You might need to hold an object or point to a picture to sustain his attention.

- Try having the student repeat the request or direction. This is not a strategy to be used all the time, however, sometimes the repetition can help a student process the information to begin an action or response.

- Determine when to repeat a request. One of the most common questions is, "How do you know how long to wait?" Your observations need to tell you. If a child looks as if he is attending, processing or thinking it seems reasonable to wait a bit longer. If he is beginning to look distracted or begins a response that is obviously incorrect, then it is time to repeat.

9. Guide or prompt the student to respond *if needed*

After you wait, you may decide he needs some prompting to help him respond. It is a bit like jump starting the battery in a car. Once the battery gets that charge of electricity it will run fine. It just may not have enough energy to get started in the beginning. That is what children can seem like. Guides or prompts can be simple and subtle like the following:

- Physical guides:

  - move an object (i.e., when you tell him to sit down, push the chair a bit in his direction)

  - point to the place he needs to look

  - turn his head a bit

  - touch his hand or arm to gently move it in the direction of the action he needs to take

  - hand him a picture or object to help him get started

- Prompts to improve the student's ability to respond verbally:

  - move your mouth in the same movement the student needs to do

  - vocalize the beginning sound of the answer the student needs to give

  - begin a sentence and then pause for the student to fill in the blank (i.e. You say, "I want_____" and then pause for him to say the rest)

  - show an object or picture or a choice of several to help the student retrieve the word he is trying to use

The challenge is to *wait* first, so you do not guide or prompt too much or too soon. There is a delicate balance between helping enough so the child can participate successfully and holding back enough so he can perform as independently as possible.

10. Stay with the interaction until you reach a desired response

We live such a fast paced life-style that it is common to move quickly from one activity to another. Microwaves, drive-thru restaurants, remote controls and fast computers reduce our tolerance for anything that does not happen quickly. Effectively interacting with our students who have communication challenges requires a change from our speedy approach to the rest of life. Moving on too quickly will eliminate many teachable moments. It is easy to ignore incorrect responses, help students too quickly, or not allow enough time for the whole communication exchange to occur. Pause. Consider each communication interaction a potential teaching opportunity. Then, when you encounter a difficult situation, be ready to slow the pace a bit so you can implement some procedures that can make a difference.

- Correct errors immediately by taking the time to show or tell the student his error.

- Modify *your* communication as needed.

- Enlist the visual supports you need to help the student be successful.

- Give "closure" to the interaction so both you and the student will know it has ended successfully. A smile, a gesture, or verbal encouragement can help a student realize his success.

Modifying our own communication style is not easy. Observe what works with a student. Once you identify some techniques that help a student become a better participator, remember to use them. You will not need to use all these strategies all the time. As you learn to integrate these techniques into your own communication style, you will develop a more effective connection. Be warned. Those things on this list that are most difficult for you to do are probably the strategies that will help your student the most.

Use Lots of Gestures!

Be a mime! Use lots of gestures when you communicate to the students. Teach them to use these gestures when communicating to everyone else. Exaggerate. Remember that gestures are visual. Make it fun!

- nod your head *yes* or shake your head *no*
- hold out your hand when you are asking for something
- point to the object you are talking about
- point to the location you are referring to
- shrug your shoulders when you say "I don't know"
- put your finger over your lips to indicate quiet
- exaggerate your facial expression to indicate surprise or anger
- put your hands over your ears to indicate too loud
- push something out of the way when you are rejecting it
- wrinkle your nose to indicate "yuck" or that something tastes bad
- make your face look surprised
- make your face look sad
- put your hands on your hips, fold your arms or shake your finger to indicate anger
- put your hand on a body part to indicate something hurts
- put your hand on your stomach to indicate you are hungry
- squeeze your nose to acknowledge something smells

To make your gestures most effective, remember these tips:

- Exaggerate your movements
- Hold your movements for a moment while the student establishes attention
- Slower, more pronounced movements will be easier for the student to understand than quick or rapidly moving ones.

THE POINT IS: Your body is a very important visual tool.

- Using gestures when you communicate can help students understand better

- Students who learn to use gestures effectively become better communicators

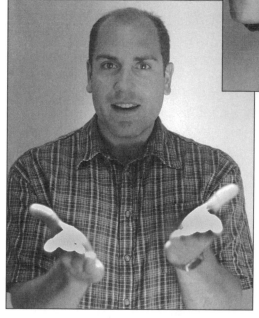

Sign language is sometimes taught to students as a form of communication. It is visual. Some students benefit from learning signs. The problem with sign language is most people don't know signs. It is a form of communication that does not work well for a lot of students. The greater number of signs a student uses, the fewer people will understand what he is attempting to communicate. Manual signs may require rapid movements which can make it difficult for students to read them. Common gestures, on the other hand, are universally understood. Students benefit from understanding and using common gestures. That is a form of communication most people will understand and use.

Chapter

6

Seven Critical Communication Skills To Teach

Of course speech is a desirable goal for students, but there are other skills that are even more critical for students to become effective communicators. Whether or not a student can speak, developing the following social and pragmatic skills needs to be considered a part of his communication training program if he does not have adequate ability in these areas.

I am a Speech Therapist, but I was trained to teach speech and language skills. This isn't speech or language.

Many Speech Therapists and teachers are not trained to understand the significance of these types of social and pragmatic skills. Their orientation is to try to teach the students to talk. For these students, that is like trying to build a house by putting the roof on before the foundation and walls are constructed. Even when students do learn to talk, they won't be effective communicators unless these skills are integrated into their communication systems.

This is different from the type of therapy I have done in the past.

That is why teaching or providing therapy for students with autism spectrum disorders is different from working with other students. Most other students don't need to learn skills in these same areas.

In fact, this is an area where parents and therapists can encounter conflict. When one of them sees the need for training in *social and pragmatic skills* and the other one is focusing more on *speech & language,* there will be disagreement. These are two different sets of skills. They intertwine, yet they are taught differently. This conflict becomes stronger when students have behavior problems because it is easy to think:

> *"If only he could talk, then he wouldn't behave like this."*

Trying to push the development of speech without teaching the supporting skills will not accomplish the goal. Remember, even if students can talk, they may still need training in social and pragmatic skills.

Developing social and pragmatic skills is a foundation for communication, no matter what verbal or non-verbal forms the student learns. These skills are essential for becoming an effective communication partner. They are foundations for appropriate behavior. Difficulty in these areas can be a significant reason many behavior problems exist. As a student becomes more capable in these skill areas, behavior will improve and the use of visual tools to support behavior will be much more effective. As you consider these abilities, *think visual!* Each skill on the list can have a strong visual framework.

1. Social Engagement

Social connection and playful interaction are skills that are frequently missing or weak in students with autism. (Students with other disabilities tend to be more skilled in this area.) If the student does not perceive other people to be valuable as communication partners, there will be no communication. The student needs to recognize other people as interesting and important. He needs to demonstrate some desire to connect, or at least respond to the interaction attempts of others.

Although any student with moderate to severe communication disorders may demonstrate a lack of competence in at least some of these skill areas, the difficulties will be most prevalent in students with autism spectrum disorders.

Stewart sees someone with a cookie. If he wants the cookie, he looks at it and hits his head. No one realizes that is a way that he is attempting to make a request. Although he is attempting to demonstrate communicative intent, other people do not understand it. Stewart needs to learn to use some different forms of communication to help people understand he is trying to make a request. For example: Teaching this skill may require physically prompting Stewart to point or reach or use some other gesture to indicate his desire.

Remember, pragmatic skills are those invisible skills that make communication effective.

- Start at the child's level. Frequently, people try to make a social connection at a level that is much higher than a student is capable of. It is critical to begin at the student's level. Real playful interaction may involve "leaving adulthood" and playing and acting like a child. Play may not mean pulling out the trucks and dolls. Real engagement frequently comes from one-on-one, face-to-face physical games and rough house-type play. Think of tickle games or peek-a-boo and hide-&-seek. Social engagement is the basis for communication.

2. Communicative Intent

To communicate effectively, it is necessary to do something on purpose - either a motor movement or a vocalization - to get a response or reaction from another person. Students with autism and some others with severe communication disorders may not do this very well or very frequently. When they do attempt to get reactions from other people, it may not be very clear to others that they are attempting to communicate. People may not recognize or accurately interpret their attempts. Teaching students to *intend to communicate* more frequently is an important goal. Helping them use a *greater variety of forms* so they can be understood more easily is also a significant need.

3. Use of Natural Gestures and Body Language

Even before verbal skills develop, natural gestures and body language become essential for communicating. A good gesture system is valuable for helping students get their wants and needs met. When students are able to use gestures to manipulate their environment, many behavior problems are avoided or modified.

• Specifically teach students how to use gestures.

• Demonstrate how to use gestures or physically prompt a student to use them for communication purposes.

• Consider universally understood, commonly used gestures like pointing and shaking your head, or "give me five".

• Teach students to exaggerate their gestures a bit to make them more likely to be understood.

Many students who are slow in speech development learn to use a very effective gesture system to get their wants and needs met. Students with autism don't tend to have that skill. They often require specific teaching to use gestures competently.

4. Use a Variety of Forms of Communication

Whether or not a student is verbal, he needs to have a "total" communication system. That means he needs to be able to use a variety of different forms of communication for interacting with others. A system can contain speech, gestures, written language, photos, pictures, objects and any other means to share their intentions. An effective communication system contains a variety of forms.

Sometimes adults are so intent on getting a student to talk that they don't respond to or support the student's use of other communication forms. Focusing on attempting to teach speech without supporting the development of other forms of communication may result in limited success.

5. Use Alternate Strategies to Get Wants and Needs Met

Students need to learn how to recognize a communication breakdown. If they try to communicate something to you and you don't understand, they need to learn to let you know in a different way. Encourage multiple forms of communication. Encourage the use of gestures or visual tools combined with vocalizations or verbalization.

6. Improve Communication with Visual Tools

Students need to pay attention to the visual tools you use to communicate to them. Teach them to access visual tools for information and take ownership of the visual aids that become a part of their life routines. Teach students to use visual tools and supports to help them communicate their intents to others. The visual tools will help them:

- pay attention
- establish communicative intent
- understand important life information
- support thinking skills
- clearly communicate their message
- successfully repair communication breakdowns
- stay engaged in their communication interactions

It is extremely critical to pay attention to the non-verbal forms that students use to attempt to communicate. The people who are most focused on teaching a child to talk will be the most likely to miss these communication attempts. It is not unusual to miss a lot of subtle attempts from the children. Behavior problems frequently erupt when students are trying to communicate but no one responds.

7. Stay With the Interaction Until the Goal is Achieved

When students encounter a *communication breakdown* the result can be:

- a behavior outburst

- withdrawal from the communication attempt

- inappropriate participation

> *When students don't understand, they need to let you know. Frequently they don't know how.*
> *If you don't understand them, they have a problem they don't know how to fix. Students may not know what to do if their attempts don't work. Teach them to persist. Encourage them to keep trying if you don't understand. This may not be easy to do, but helping the student use a variety of forms, particularly visual forms, to communicate will help them repair the breakdowns. When the student perceives you are attempting to understand, the behavior outbursts may be delayed long enough for the message attempt to be successful.*

Skills in these areas of communication will improve the ability of students to participate effectively in communication interactions. The more capable the students are in these support skills, the more effective the visual tools will be that are implemented to solve behavior problems.

Part 4

Using Visual Strategies to Support Communication and Solve Behavior Problems

Understanding the natural connection between communication and behavior problems is the first step to finding solutions. Recognizing the immense value of visual strategies as a means to support communication is the second critical step.

Part 4 will take you on a journey. This journey will connect the three pieces that we have been discussing: behavior problems, communication, and visual strategies. You will see how visual tools and supports are developed to improve communication and solve behavior problems.

It is helpful to talk about visual tools in categories. That will guide your thinking. You will quickly see that it can take more than one type of visual tool to completely handle situations. You will also see that there may be more than one option to use for a specific need.

The best solutions do not come in neat categories. Think of it as *Mix & Match.* When your student encounters a difficulty you may come up with several ways to handle it. Or you may develop several tools that will each support a part of the problem. Remember that behavior difficulties can be complex. *Look for the communication opportunities that are imbedded in each situation.* You will discover communication solutions for many types of behavior difficulties. Then you will view lots of Samples & Examples of situations where visual tools successfully made a difference.

Chapter

7

Visual Tools To Improve Understanding

Life is full of information. Figuring out what is happening and when can be a challenge for any person. Consider the people you know. Some are probably quite good at "going with the flow." They can handle changes and emergencies with ease. In fact, routine may be boring to them. You may know others who get tense or upset when there is too much chaos around. They are happy and cheerful when life's routines are predictable, but they fall apart easily when the unexpected pops up.

Perhaps we all like a bit of routine for at least some parts of our lives so we don't have to work so hard. When the routines are interrupted or confusion takes over, stress levels rise. We cling to familiar routines so we don't have to experience the stress of change. So do our students. For our students, behavior problems frequently emerge as the result of information breakdowns, during transitions or changes, or at other times when students don't understand or become confused.

What are information breakdowns?

When the predictable routines of life change. When students don't understand or they don't remember. When there is confusion about what to expect. Students with communication difficulties can be affected more severely in these situations than the average person. Think about your own life.

• How do you react when the mailman doesn't deliver your mail? Does it cause a problem? Do you get upset? Would it make a difference if this was the first time he forgot or if he has forgotten every day this week? What about if it was a Sunday or a holiday?

• How do you respond when someone gives you directions to find a store or doctor's office or somewhere else you need to go? You follow those directions and you end up lost. First, imagine the frustration. Then think about what you need to do to get where you are trying to go.

These are information breakdowns. They are those times when the expected routines are changed or we don't have all the information. We don't know the answers we need to handle what we need to handle. For us, these are isolated situations. For our students, all of life can feel like this.

Why are these situations so difficult for students?

Handling them requires interpreting lots of communication, the actions of other people and situations in the environment. It requires skills such as remembering past communication and events and quickly generalizing to new situations. These are all the skills that our students have difficulty with because of their disabilities. In addition, these situations tend to be highly verbal; stressing the weakest part of these student's communication systems. The result can frequently be melt down, break down, shut down or behavior outburst. Whatever way that student expresses his frustration will come out strongly.

Life can't possibly be totally routine. It is full of changes and situations that are out of everyone's control. How can you help students so they won't be so affected by information breakdowns?

You can't fix every situation. But there is a lot you can do to help. Providing support in the areas where you have some control reduces stress. When many parts of the student's life are relaxed and predictable, they have more energy and tolerance for dealing with the challenges. Here is what to do:

1. Develop a lifestyle of familiar schedules and routines

When students know what to expect and what is going on during large parts of their day they will have more tolerance for those times when things are not predictable. There is a huge difference between having to cope for a ten-minute incident and having to struggle through a whole day of confusion.

2. Communicate information to students in a form that they can understand easily

Taking the time to communicate information to a student in a *form* he understands can prevent spending a lot more time later trying to manage a behavior difficulty that erupts because the student doesn't understand.

> *Many students live their lives with a high level of stress and anxiety that is caused, at least in part, to the stress of trying to understand their life schedules and routines.*

SCHEDULES & CALENDARS

- Do you use a personal planner?

- Have you been known to write yourself messages on those little yellow sticky notes and post them in obvious places to help you remember what to do?

- Do you write important events on a calendar?

- Did you ever show up at an appointment at the wrong time because you forgot to change it on your calendar?

- Did you ever miss the appointment completely because you forgot to write it down?

I use my daily planner and those yellow sticky notes all the time! They help me keep my life sane.

Most of us use these types of systems to help organize our own lives. If these techniques are familiar to you, you will easily understand how helpful the systems can be for our students. If you have encountered problems from forgetting to use your system, you know how frustrating it can be.

But I know people who never use those tools. They just remember everything! Their brains must be awfully full!

If you are one of those people who remembers everything in your brain, you may have a harder time understanding the student's need. Be assured, it is a critical need! You will have to work harder to understand the student's learning style if it is different from your own.

Schedules and calendars help us by telling us:

- what is going to happen
- what is not going to happen
- when something is going to happen
- what is changing
- what is different
- what I have to remember
- what I don't want to forget
- what I have to look forward to
- what already occurred
- and whatever other information we put on them

A student's participation and behavior can deteriorate rapidly when he becomes confused, doesn't remember or doesn't understand. When students don't understand what is happening and when, anxiety increases. Using these tools helps us organize our thinking and organize our lives. They help the students in the same way.

HOW TO USE SCHEDULES AND CALENDARS

■ **Use schedules to tell the student what is happening now**

- the sequence of events

- what is changing

- what behavior will be expected when something happens

- repeat or rehearse what the event will be and what the student will do

■ **Use them to talk about what is going to happen in the future**

- schedules and calendars are excellent resources to guide conversation about future experiences

- use them to help the student rehearse how he will behave for a future event

■ **Use schedules and calendars to tell students when something is going to change or occur differently from what they expect.**

- prepare them for change

- let them know what will not happen

- tell them what will happen instead

- assure them the changes will be OK

■ **Combine schedules and calendars with other visual tools to rehearse:**

- what will happen

- what will not happen

- who will be there

- expected behavior

- unexpected possibilities

SAMPLES & EXAMPLES

PROBLEM: Aaron loves to go bowling. He asks, "Go bowling?" several dozen times a day.

CAUSE: Aaron asks the same questions over and over as a way of getting information that he can't remember. Those questions are also a way of attempting to have a conversation.

SOLUTION: Use a schedule to give daily information and a calendar to give longer-term information about Aaron's favorite activity. He can use both tools to help him understand how long he has to wait until the next time. Use them to help talk about when he will bowl again. In addition, Aaron needs to learn to say some other things about bowling to help him have a more extensive conversation.

SCHEDULE

8:30	Group Time
9:00	Library
9:30	Work
10:30	music
11:00	Lunch
12:00	BOWLING

S	M	T	W	TH	F	SA
1	2	3	4	5	6 BOWLING	7
8	9	10	11	12	13 BOWLING	14
15	16	17	18	19	20	21

PROBLEM: Art is involved in a community-based job training program. He loves his job and eagerly participates. There are some days that he cannot go to the job site because of scheduling changes. If he can't go, he becomes very angry.

CAUSE: It appears that Art thinks he is being punished when he can't go to his job. He doesn't understand the changes in schedule.

SOLUTION: Use a schedule and calendar to give him the information about the work schedule. Write down the information he needs to understand.

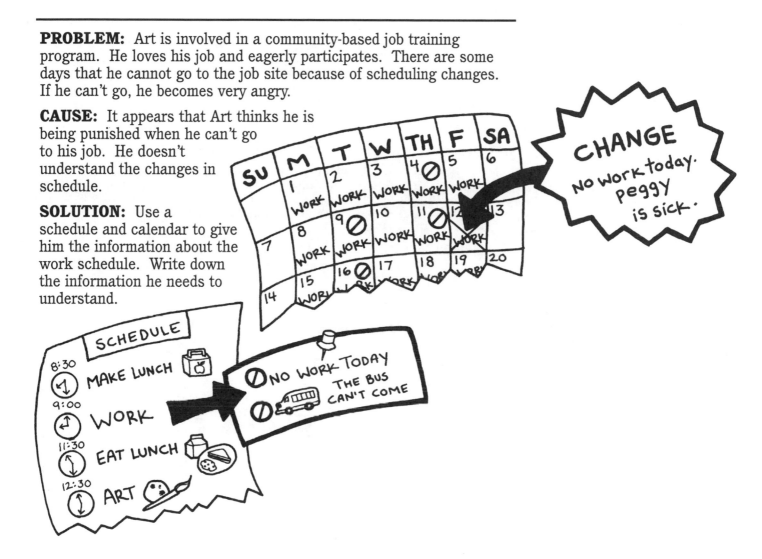

PROBLEM: Timmy has a hard time getting ready for school. Mom has to nag him constantly. He will be sitting in his underwear watching TV when he should be dressed and eating breakfast. He is always forgetting part of his grooming routine. Mom thinks he is old enough and capable enough to become more independent with these routines.

CAUSE: Timmy just doesn't remember. He gets distracted easily by his toys and the TV. He doesn't have a good sense of time to help him know when things should be done.

SOLUTION: Develop a schedule for his morning routine. Teach Timmy to follow the schedule. Use a timer or a clock to help him stay on task and better gage the length of time he is taking to complete his routine. Let him know that if he gets everything done there will be time to watch TV until the bus comes.

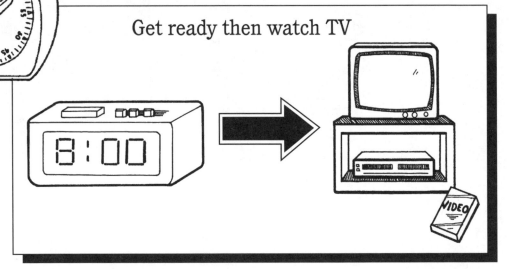

Get ready then watch TV

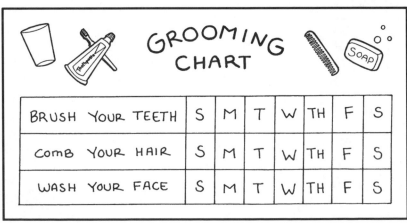

GROOMING CHART

BRUSH YOUR TEETH	S	M	T	W	TH	F	S
COMB YOUR HAIR	S	M	T	W	TH	F	S
WASH YOUR FACE	S	M	T	W	TH	F	S

THE POINT IS: Schedules and calendars can:

- Give students information about their lives

- Prepare students for what will or will not happen

- Reduce the anxiety that comes from the unexpected, especially during transition times

- Help students understand when something is completed or finished

- Support communication and conversation

- Provide the structure for appropriate behavior and participation

Schedules are tools to use to tell students what is expected right now in the present. They help direct the student about where to go, what to do, or what objects to get. Use the schedule to tell the student what is happening. Then guide him to show him what that means. It is essential to teach the student what the schedule item means if he doesn't understand what action to take. This is especially critical for younger students or those who are just learning what a schedule is.

> *Think about the anxiety you experience when your life becomes unpredictable. Stress. These students can live in a constant state of stress.*

> *Most of the visual tools in this book are opportunities to give students information. Don't worry if there seems to be a lot of overlap. Think about the function or purpose for the tool. That is what is important.*

TOOLS TO GIVE INFORMATION ABOUT LIFE

The most common way we give information to students is verbally. We *tell* them what we want them to know. Unfortunately, listening is not their most efficient system of understanding.

What kind of information are you talking about?

Any information. Just think of all the things we tell students and then expect them to understand and remember.

- what is happening
- who is doing something
- when it will occur
- what they need to remember
- what is expected to happen in the future

This sounds like the information we share in conversation.

It is. But the problem is, our students don't necessarily completely or adequately understand the ongoing conversation. They don't comprehend the *information of life* that is going on around them. That is where real behavior problems begin to emerge.

Why do behavior problems develop?

Because people think students know what is happening. They:

- *assume* the students understand the same way everyone else does
- *presume* the students are understanding the ongoing conversations and routines
- *expect* students to remember information that was given previously

What can be worse is when people:

- *assume* it is not important to tell the student
- *presume* the student won't understand
- *don't see the relationship* between behavior that the student produces and the fact that he does not understand what is happening

Behavior problems emerge because what the student is expecting and what is really happening are not the same. Think about it. Students generally don't *intend* to be bad, but from their point of view much of life is a big surprise. They frequently don't have adequate communication skills to get the information they need to help them understand. They respond to situations using what understanding they do have or what they remember from past events. When that doesn't work, they use whatever means they have to try to gain some control. That can be why they cling to predictable routines and resist change. Giving them information about what is happening is a critical need for them to successfully manage the ebb and flow of life.

How do you recommend sharing more information?

Think of the things that you are apt to share in conversation. Then think about making your conversations more visual. Schedules and calendars give information about the big pieces of life. Conversations fill in the details.

Do you mean I have to have a picture for everything I say?

It isn't that bad! How much you share and how you do it will depend on the age and ability level of your student. Younger students and lower skilled students will comprehend a different amount of information than older students and those with more communication skill. It's important to match the amount of information you share with what the student needs and can understand. Giving too much can be as problematic as not giving enough. Give students the information they *want to know* and the information they *need to know* in a *form* they understand. Look at these examples.

> *Sometimes adults just forget to communicate with students. This can be particularly evident when students are non-verbal or have limited communication skills. Because the students don't talk, the adults forget to tell them things.*

SAMPLES & EXAMPLES

PROBLEM: Mom needs to go to the grocery store. JD is playing his favorite video game. Mom knows it is going to be a struggle to get JD to come with her. She knows he has difficulty with transitions.

CAUSE: Mom doesn't prepare JD for what she wants to do. She walks over and turns off the video game and tells JD they are going to the store. JD resists. Why? It is not difficult to figure out why. First, he was enjoying his favorite game. Second, he doesn't really know what is going to be happening after he is removed from his activity. He doesn't know where he is going, what will be happening or when he can play video again.

SOLUTION: Mom needs to plan ahead a bit. Look at the list of things she could choose from to make this a less challenging situation:

1. Use a daily schedule or a calendar to indicate grocery shopping.

2. Use a card to tell JD what time shopping will be.

3. Show JD a picture of the grocery store. Show him what you will be doing or buying there.

4. Have him help prepare the shopping list of what will be purchased.

5. Write a little story that tells JD what will be happening.

6. Set a timer to prepare him for the change. Let him know they will be leaving in 5 or 10 minutes or whenever the timer goes off.

7. Develop a "going to the store" routine. Visually show him the steps necessary to get ready to leave for the store.

Won't it take a lot of time to plan ahead to prepare JD for the shopping trip?

Yes, it will take a little time, but it will probably take less time to give him information than it will to deal with the difficult behavior that will likely occur otherwise. Mom does not have to do all the things on the list. These are just suggestions and Mom may actually be able to think of several more. To make it work Mom needs to:

Think ahead.

Start a collection of visuals to help transition situations so they are there when she needs them. (Once you begin a collection of visual tools, save them so you can use them over and over.)

Use visual tools to help give JD information instead of just telling him.

THE POINT IS: Mom needs to give JD information in a form that he understands to prepare him for the shopping trip.

For younger children a very simple approach would be to use two pictures; one picture of what the child is doing now and one picture of where you are going. Put a NO sign on the picture of what the child is currently doing or turn the picture over. Then show the child what you are doing next. Hand it to him to hold while you are moving to the next activity.

Create a collection of pictures and other visuals to support your communication. File card boxes, 3-ring binders, pocket photo albums and other holders make good storage places for them. Magnets on the refrigerator make convenient holders. Then you always know where they are. You don't need to have everything at once. Let your collection grow as you encounter different needs.

GOING TO SUPER KMART

PUSH THE SHOPPING CART

BUY ONLY WHAT IS ON THE SHOPPING LIST

NO SUPER NINTENDO TODAY

CHECK OUT

CHOOSE A SNACK

PROBLEM: Kevin is really excited because he just got $20.00 in his birthday card. He declared he wants to go to Super Kmart to spend it. Dad knows that when they get to the store Kevin will fixate on the expensive video games that cost much more money than he has. Dad is expecting a tantrum in the store.

CAUSE: Kevin doesn't understand money concepts. When you tell him at home what he can or cannot buy, he doesn't understand and remember in a way that helps in the store. Once he actually sees those expensive games, he is out of control. Dad wants Kevin to have the shopping experience, but he isn't sure how to handle the potential problem.

SOLUTION: Give Kevin lots of information ahead of time to prepare him for what will happen in the store. Dad could try these ideas:

1. Make a shopping list with Kevin.

2. Show Kevin what choices he will have when he goes to the store.

3. Show Kevin what will not happen today (no video games today).

4. Make a schedule of what will happen in the store so there is no time to go to the video game department.

5. Write a story that tells Kevin what will happen.

Dad could try any of these ideas or a combination of them. *The critical part will be following through with what the visual information says.* If Dad gives Kevin a card that says, "no looking at video games" then he can't take Kevin over to look at the video games. If the rule is "no buying a video game today", Dad better not come home with one. Even if Kevin has a tantrum. Dad has to honor what the card says and follow the information given to Kevin. Otherwise, Kevin will be confused and he won't understand the true meaning behind the visual supports. Even if Kevin has a hard time today it is important to stick with it so he will learn for the next time.

If Dad really expects difficulties he should plan ahead for a backup. For example:

- Have more than one visual tool to explain different aspects of the situation.

- Plan to stay in the store a very short time. This may not be the day for browsing or other shopping.

- Plan something highly desirable to occur right after the store so there will be a reason to get done and leave. Of course, have a visual tool to show Kevin what that is.

THE POINT IS: Giving information in a visual form will help Kevin understand what will happen and what will not happen.

PROBLEM: Jason just started buying hot lunch in the cafeteria. The first day he had several behavior outbursts. His behaviors included screaming, biting his hand, slapping the glass around the food, pushing his tray off the table and a few other similar actions.

CAUSE: Jason didn't like the food that the cook put on his plate. He protested, however, his strategies were not appropriate. He didn't understand that he didn't have to eat it.

SOLUTION: First, it is necessary to determine if Jason has a choice about what goes on his lunch plate.

If Jason does have a choice:

• look at the menu ahead of time to give him information about what will be there

• help him learn to make an appropriate request

• teach him ways to reject something he doesn't want in an acceptable fashion (something that means "no thank you").

If the lunch servers do not accommodate for individual choices:

• Jason needs to learn to accept what he is given

• he needs to learn what to do about the food he doesn't want or like

THE POINT IS: Jason is facing a daily situation that can cause daily difficulties. He needs information to help him know what to expect and how to handle the situation.

Eating Lunch

Sit down 	Be quiet
Eat the food you want 	Don't touch the food you don't want 
Be quiet 	Don't talk about the food you don't want 
At 11:25 throw away the food you don't like 	

**Tuesday
Hot Lunch Menu**

Sloppy Joe
French Fries
Green Beans
Peaches
Milk

Say: No Green Beans Please

PROBLEM: Stacey's mom was taking her to the doctor for a check-up. Stacey began to cry and bite her wrist. She kept yelling, "No shot!" while she pounded her head with her fist. Her behavior escalated, making it difficult for Mom to try to get her into the car.

CAUSE: Even though mom told Stacey she was not going to get a shot this time, Stacey was nervous because she remembered her last trip there. She remembered getting a shot that hurt the last time she went to the doctor. Stacey needs a lot of information. Her memory of fear and pain surfaced. She doesn't have enough language to really discuss the situation. Therefore, she expressed her fear with protest and crying.

SOLUTION: Giving Stacey information will help her anticipate the event. Learning more vocabulary would help her avoid the extreme reaction of fear. There are several ways to handle this situation.

Give Stacey information about what will be happening:

- Tell her verbally and visually where she is going

- Let her know the sequence of events

- Give her information about what will happen and what will not happen

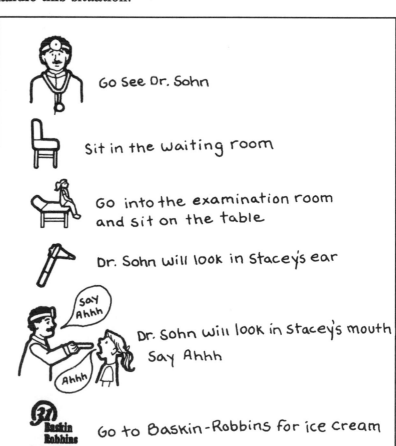

Go See Dr. Sohn

Sit in the waiting room

Go into the examination room and sit on the table

Dr. Sohn will look in Stacey's ear

Dr. Sohn will look in Stacey's mouth Say Ahhh

Go to Baskin-Robbins for ice cream

Since Stacey is apt to echo the phrases you are stating, try to state them in a form that will be appropriate when she repeats them. Using pronouns can be confusing for many. If students are able to use personal pronouns (I, me, mine, etc.) appropriately, then you can use them. If the student still demonstrates confusion with this language skill, try using her name to avoid confusion. It is too frustrating to sort out pronoun selection during a time of stress.

Give Stacey information with calming or reassuring phrases that she can repeat. Support them visually:

Holding a picture and repeating phrases helps a student focus on something positive. This has a way of helping the student regulate her own behavior.

> "It is OK to go to the doctor."

> "The doctor is funny."

> "The doctor helps Stacey feel better."

> "No shot today."

> "The nurse gives Stacey a sucker."

Write it down:

Writing phrases down will help Stacey remember them and rehearse them. Stacey will learn scripts like these when they are repeated while preparing her for the event. Even if she memorizes them or echoes them, they will be a reasonable starting place to have a conversation about the situation. Even if Stacey perseverates and repeats one of these phrases a number of times, it is a way of giving her something appropriate to say about the situation.

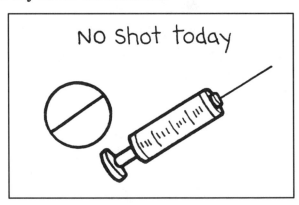

No Shot today

Give choices of things to say or do:

Try giving Stacey a list of some other things to say or do when she is encountering this situation.

> **Things to do when I go to the doctor's office:**
>
> • Hold mom's hand
> • Read my book
> • Say, "I am nervous"
> • Think about the mermaid video
> • Take 5 deep breaths
> • Say "No shot today"
> • Say "It's going to be OK"

If she really will get a shot, try giving specific information:

> • "Stacey can hold her blanket when the doctor gives the shot."
>
> • "The shot will pinch just a little bit. Stacey says 'Ouch! I don't like it!' Then it's all finished. Then go for ice cream."

In theory, as Stacey rehearses the various language choices or reads the information with you she will begin to absorb or take on the attitude that those tools present. Any combination of these options can help Stacey understand better what is happening and help her learn more things to say about the event. Having a greater variety of things to say will give Stacey the opportunity to modify her behavior

NOTE: *Timing* is important when preparing students for events. How much time you give a student to prepare may depend on how good or bad the student perceives the event to be.

- Sometimes adults wait until just before an event to give the student information about it. In some circumstances that can be good because a student may be anxious and perseverate on the topic. Their behavior may actually escalate from anxiety during the waiting period.

- Some students need more time to process the information to get ready for an event. They benefit from multiple conversations and mentally rehearsing the event. Be sure to give these students enough time to prepare. Remember that preparation time is also an excellent communication training time.

THE POINT IS: Using visual tools to give information to students is a way of preparing them. First, we have to remember to give them information. Then we need to give that information in forms that they understand easily. When students understand what is happening they are more likely to participate successfully.

C h a p t e r

Strategies To Help Students Control Their Environments

One of the most important stages of communication development is when children reach the point where they can purposefully control their environment. They learn two critical skills:

- how to make it clear what they *don't* want

- what to do to let you know what they *do* want

Acquiring the vocabulary and other communication skills to make requests and developing their ability to communicate the infamous word *no* are monumental accomplishments. In typical development, the stage of the "terrible two's" represents the height of this struggle to gain power over the world.

How do children learn the power of communication?

Through trial and error, children begin to learn what works. They practice using many communication *forms* to accomplish their goals. A child experiments by using combinations of gestures, emerging language, and behaviors to communicate. When he gets what he wants, he begins to remember what he needed to do to accomplish that goal. Then, the next time he has a need, he is more apt to use a strategy that worked the last time. Children who used to be compliant and interactive suddenly seem to change. They certainly seem to master letting you know what they *don't* want! This stage can be painfully discouraging for parents.

Do children with communication difficulties accomplish this same stage of development?

Most of them do, however, there can be some major differences. One significant difference can be the *timing* of this stage of development. When children are delayed in developing effective communication skills, they may not accomplish this "acquisition of power" until they are three or four or seven or older. What can appear to be an emerging behavior problem in a student who is older than two may really be the emergence of a powerful new stage of communication development. When these children have tantrums, parents describe their behavior as bratty, obstinate, headstrong, or willful. Instead of "being bad", they may really be attempting to master some new skills.

If these students are developing more communication skills, why does their behavior appear to get worse?

Remember, we said that children would experiment by using a variety of communication *forms*? They will try to use whatever has worked to help them reach their goals in the past, even temper tantrums. Students with communication disorders may not use the most *effective* or *appropriate* forms of communication to get their needs met. They may not use the same forms that other students do. People in their lives may actually reward or respond to inappropriate behaviors that are used as a means of communication.

Why would people reward inappropriate behaviors?

Because they don't realize that is what they are doing. They may actually be reinforcing the problem behavior they are trying to stop. Here are some examples:

- Bethany started to grab the cookies. Mom said, "No cookies before dinner," as she put them away. Bethany began to tantrum. . . .lots of crying and flailing on the floor. When Mom tried to get her to stop, it just escalated the child's protest. The only way mom felt she could stop the tantrum was to give Bethany a cookie. The next time Bethany wanted a cookie, can you guess what strategy she used to get it?

- Jason ran up to adults and pounded them on the back with his fists. When he was hitting, the adults would grab him, put him on their laps and hug him with a huge bear hug to stop his attacks. They began to observe that Jason really appeared to like those bear hugs. Perhaps Jason thought those bear hugs were desirable. It was finally decided that his hitting might not be a form of aggression, but rather an inappropriate way of requesting a hug. Once Jason was taught to hold out his arms to request a hug in a more conventional manner, the hitting diminished.

These are just two examples where the students are communicating their desires inappropriately. The *forms* they are using to communicate what they want are not the typical or expected or desirable forms that children use to accomplish those desires. The adult response to those communication attempts actually reinforced or encouraged the inappropriate communication and behavior.

What recommendations do you have for improving communication to help these students gain more appropriate control in their environment?

They are letting us know what they want, but the strategies they use may not be the most appropriate or the most effective. Students need to learn appropriate ways to communicate their wants and needs. Other students seem to learn these skills naturally, without any instruction. Our targeted students may need to be specifically taught how to accomplish them. Important skills to teach include:

- making choices
- making requests
- using appropriate strategies to reject what they don't want
- language and skills to negotiate life

Let's explore how to teach these skills.

MAKING CHOICES AND REQUESTS

One of the *first* skills that can be effectively taught to students with communication difficulties or those who are emerging in developing communication skills is how to make choices. This is a great place to begin early training because:

- Students are *more likely to pay attention* when the choices are highly desirable.

- It is fairly easy to *structure* a choice-making interaction.

- Presenting choices encourages students to have a *strong desire to participate*.

- The student will have a *strong motivation to communicate* if the choices are highly desirable.

- Passive students are more likely to indicate a desire to participate.

- Students will demonstrate *more effort to stay involved* in a social interaction that will enable them to get what they want.

- Using highly desirable choices gives students *immediate reinforcement* for their efforts.

- Students have an *opportunity to control* what they get.

- This skill *can be practiced multiple times a day,* which facilitates more rapid learning than when skills occur less frequently.

- Adults can *structure the choices* that are available.

Our own lives are filled with opportunities to make choices. Particularly parents of young children don't realize how necessary it is to allow their children this opportunity to become independent. Think of snack time. Some parents feel like it is spoiling children to give them that much control over what they get. Other parents feel like this is one area when they (the parents) can actually feel successful with their children. Feeding them is something that works when there are lots of times during the day that are much more frustrating. Whatever the issue, it needs to be recognized that choice making offers a wonderful opportunity to teach communication.

Some people think it is not a good idea to give choices to students. Why don't people want to give them choices?

- The adults are afraid they will *lose control*, particularly if the student is difficult to deal with.

- There is a *fear* that giving students choices will make them bossy or controlling or out of control. This feeds into the adult worries about having a *student* who is the one *in charge*.

- There is a fear that giving students choices will *make the adults powerless* or that the student will not "mind" the adult anymore.

- Adults feel like they *already know* what the child wants anyway.

- Adults may think it is *easier* not to give choices.

- Students may make choices that are not available or not appropriate.

- Students make choices but don't really want what they choose and that causes behavior incidents.

- There is fear that the student will make choices that the adult doesn't approve of.

- Adults have concerns that the student will not choose what is good for him.

- Students may be perceived to be too young, too low skilled, not ready yet, or incapable for some other reason.

- Perhaps *no one thought of trying* to give the student a choice.

Do you recommend allowing students to make choices?

In spite of the concerns that some people have, giving students opportunities to make choices is a critically valuable strategy for encouraging cooperation and positive participation. It is a way that children begin to learn that they have power over what happens in their lives. That creates a high level of motivation to communicate in appropriate ways. It teaches students to replace inappropriate behaviors with more acceptable ways to get what they want.

How often should students be allowed to choose? Shouldn't there be times when they need to follow whatever the requirements or rules are?

Of course! This is not a suggestion that everything in life should be optional. There are times when there is no choice. Everything is not negotiable. Wisdom knows the difference.

How can making choices help behavior situations?

Here are two ways:

- Many times protests or behavior outbursts occur because the child is just emerging in his ability to manipulate what is happening and he has not yet reached a level of successful communication. There are occasions where offering choices can avoid confrontations or resistance. Offering just one option may not satisfy the student as well as offering more than one choice.

- When there is a situation where the student cannot have nor do what he desires, offering alternative choices can circumvent the protest and help him transition into an alternate activity more easily.

Providing some options gives students an opportunity to participate in their own destiny. As communication partners, how we respond to these situations aids students in developing more effective skills. Let's look at some examples:

SAMPLES & EXAMPLES

PROBLEM: Remember Bethany (above) who was having tantrums because she wanted a cookie? She was communicating clearly to Mom what she wanted. Mom didn't want her to have a cookie before dinner.

CAUSE: Since children's tummies and the dinner clock don't always coordinate, it is very reasonable that Bethany was hungry. Perhaps she didn't understand how long she was going to have to wait for dinner. She probably didn't understand the concept of waiting. Her sense of hunger was probably immediate and the only thing she knew to do was to try to satisfy that hunger.

2 food choices

banana

drink

SOLUTION: Even though Mom wants Bethany to wait until dinner to eat, enduring a tantrum until dinner could be torture. Mom could decide to give Bethany a choice of something more appropriate for a before dinner snack. A fruit or vegetable, a drink of water or an early portion of dinner are possibilities. If Mom just gives one thing to Bethany, that may or may not be acceptable from the child's point of view. If Bethany is determined to get a cookie, she may not relinquish easily. Giving her a choice of two or three items may placate her more. Another strategy Mom can use is to show Bethany visually that she can have her cookie after dinner, if that will be an acceptable option. Many times students will relinquish the immediate desire when given other options. Telling her *when* she can have what she wants helps her accept the situation.

PROBLEM: Joey was learning to independently tell his teachers that he needed to go to the bathroom. Every time he would request the bathroom, one of the teaching staff would walk with him to go there down the hall. They began to notice that Joey was requesting to go to the bathroom more and more frequently. In addition, it was observed that when he got to the bathroom he frequently didn't have to go. They began to question this situation. Why did he keep asking to go there if he didn't need to use the bathroom?

CAUSE: Wise observers began to notice that Joey appeared to really like that walk down the hall. He wasn't in a hurry. He looked at things and talked about things. That walk was a great pleasure to him. The hypothesis developed: Joey wasn't making all those requests so he could go to the bathroom. Perhaps he was really requesting to go for a walk down the hall. Requesting the bathroom was the only way he knew how to make that happen.

SOLUTION: The teacher decided to make *going for a walk* one of Joey's choices after he finished his work. Once Joey had a way to choose *going for a walk*, the requests for the bathroom reduced to only those times of real need. Once the walk option was presented, it became Joey's favorite reward for good work.

Walk

Bathroom

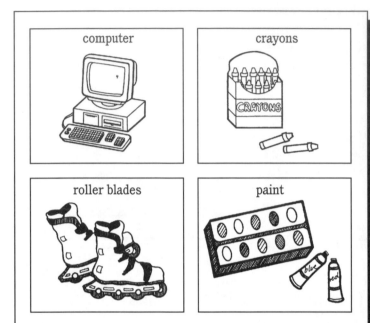

PROBLEM: Cindy was not a cooperative worker. Whenever her aide tried to sit down with her to do structured, teacher assigned schoolwork, Cindy's protest became creative and strong. She had a long list of behaviors that produced scratches and bruises on others. There were other activities, however, that Cindy loved to do. She would stay involved for long periods of time for her desired activities.

CAUSE: Cindy had developed a pattern of protesting whatever was requested of her. It didn't matter what you wanted her to do.

SOLUTION: It was decided that the first goal was to develop some positive "work sessions" with Cindy. A choice board was created with several of her highly desired activities. Cindy was given the opportunity to choose which activities she was going to do. Then in her structured work setting she was guided to follow the sequence she had created. Of course, she was eager to do the activities because she had chosen them. This created greater cooperation because the structured time was highly motivating from Cindy's point of view.

→ Reward

SOLUTION 2: After Cindy's participation improved, the teacher began using Cindy's choices as a reward. The teacher would choose one activity and Cindy could choose the reward that would follow.

The teacher began to interject a greater variety of work skills that she wanted Cindy to participate in. Cindy would tolerate the teacher-initiated choices better when she knew she would be able to follow with something of her choosing. When the teacher introduced this variation, she started out by making the teacher activities quite short. As Cindy's cooperation increased, the teacher activities became longer. Eventually, the teacher changed the sequence so Cindy had to participate in two teacher chosen activities before earning her choice. (You might call that bribery!) But through all this, being able to choose her favorite activities rewarded Cindy's cooperation.

PROBLEM: Gerald is one of those passive students who doesn't seem to care about or desire much. His teacher decided to try to get more initiation and participation from him by giving him some food choices. He loves to eat and will eat anything. He seems satisfied with any snack food the teacher gives him. If she holds up two choices, Gerald will reach out to try to take both things.

apple

shoes

CAUSE: The teacher feels he is just reaching and grabbing without looking or really paying attention to what she has. Since he eats anything, it doesn't matter to him what he grabs, as long as it is food. The teacher's challenge is to get Gerald to pay attention more and to make more selective choices.

SOLUTION: The teacher decided to make a change in what choices she was offering. If she offered Gerald two food items, he really didn't care what he got. Either item was equally desirable to him. Instead, she decided to offer him a food item along with another item that was not food. For the second choice, she selected a "non item"; something that Gerald would not have any interest in. That caused Gerald to pay more attention. When he grabbed something that was not food, he realized his stomach was not being fed. Then he began to look more so he could make sure he was getting food.

TEACH STUDENTS WHAT IT MEANS TO MAKE A CHOICE OR REQUEST

After hearing a discussion about choice making, Mom was excited to try this new concept with Jason. They went to a restaurant that had lots of pictures on the menu. In the past, Mom would just order for Jason. This time, instead of ordering for him, Mom took the time to look at the pictures with him and asked him what he wanted for lunch. Jason pointed to spaghetti. When the food came, Jason looked at his plate and then eyed Mom's french fries. He kept reaching for Mom's fries and didn't touch his spaghetti. At this point, Mom was ready to give up on giving Jason choices because she ordered him something that he didn't eat.

Why didn't it work when Mom gave Jason a choice?

She didn't *teach* him what it means to make a choice. If making a choice is a new skill for Jason, he has to understand what the result of that action is. Think about the understandings and confusions that can evolve as a part of learning what it means to make a choice.

- When you choose something, that means *you get what you choose.*

- When you choose one thing, *does it mean that you reject the other choices?*

- Does it mean you are *"stuck"* with what you choose?

- Can you have *more than one choice?*

- Can you choose *both or all* the options?

- After you make a choice, *can you change your mind?*

- What happens if you choose something and *you do not get what you thought you were going to get?*

- What happens when you make *a choice that you don't like* for some reason?

- If something else looks better than what you picked, *can you change your mind?*

- When is it OK to request or *choose again?*

- When do you get *only one chance?*

I didn't think making choices was so complicated!

For some students it isn't complicated. They just "get it." They understand. But, many students can encounter problems. Even though choice making seems like a simple skill, it can become particularly confusing when students do not have the communication understandings or language skills to manipulate the rules. We, as adults, understand all kinds of arbitrary rules that change depending on the specific situation. Remember that those unwritten rules don't make sense to students. Think about the confusing thoughts that can be going on inside one of those student's brains:

> *Confusion is compounded because adults are not always consistent in their handling of student desires.*

- Why is it that sometimes I can have all the choices and at other times I am limited to only one? (At home they let me make lots of choices but in the restaurant they only let me make one.)

- Sometimes I can change my mind and at other times I am not allowed to.

- Why do the pictures look different from the real thing?

- Why don't they understand I won't eat this because it tastes different from what I am used to. . . or because there is parsley on the plate. . . . or because it is cooked a different way?

- Why do you let me have more peas when I choose them again but you don't let me have another cookie when I choose that again?

- You are giving me a choice but you are not giving me the opportunity to choose what I really want.

Think about how you browse through the options at your favorite ice cream store. Even if your most beloved flavor is vanilla, do you find yourself eyeing all the containers to see what is there? Even if you end up ordering vanilla, you are satisfied because you had a chance to look to see what else was a possibility. Oh-oh. . . .wait a minute. . . .they have chocolate-butter rum-nut-tin cup-cherry-gobble-de-gook ice cream! Hold that order! I changed my mind!

Sometimes students are very repetitive in their selections. Perhaps they only like one thing. Another possibility is that they don't know what the other options are.,,They may not really understand what it means to make a choice. They may actually think they are supposed to find the same item every time. Here is a technique to try if the student chooses the same item all the time. Make sure the choices are visual...pictures, objects or whatever. The first time, let him choose his favorite item. When it is time for him to choose again, make the first choice unavailable. Cover it up, turn it over, move it out of reach or some other strategy to indicate that one is used or finished or not available any more. Then suggest making a choice from the rest of the selections. Keep following this procedure until all the options are tried.

TECHNIQUES TO TEACH CHOICE MAKING

Although some students seem to naturally understand what it means to make a choice, others need to be specifically taught what it means.

1. Use visual choices

Visually show the student what is available. When working with very young children, lower skilled students or students who are just emerging in the development of choice-making skills, the initial teaching may be more effective when using real objects. Objects, pictures or written words are appropriate for students who understand them easily. Use whatever form the student will understand.

2. Begin by presenting two choices

Place the choices in front of the student. Ask the student, "Do you want an apple or banana?" When you name each item, move it toward the child or hold it out a bit to emphasize what you are presenting.

3. Encourage the child to indicate his choice

Decide what forms of communication you would like the student to use to make his choice. The goal is to encourage whatever combination of forms of communication the student is capable of using. To reach that goal you may need to encourage:

- touching or pointing to his choice

- handing you a picture of his choice

- combining his gestures or pictures with vocalizations or words

Do not exasperate your children. Expecting forms of communication that are too difficult for the students can actually increase behavior incidents. In the beginning, you may need to accept what they can do to make a choice. As they begin to learn the procedure, you can gradually expect more sophisticated forms of communication to request the choice.

When teaching students to indicate their choices, gradually teach the student to use a *variety of forms* to make that request or choice. If you only teach one form, it will be more difficult to generalize that skill into real life situations where you may not have as much control over the environment.

4. Give the student what he chooses

5. Move or remove the item that was not chosen

Receiving what was chosen produces satisfaction. Sometimes students don't understand that choosing one item means rejecting the other. Moving or removing the other item clarifies that concept.

Another variation is to focus on teaching a student to initiate making a request. Teach him to hand you a picture to request an item he wants. The system begins like this:

- place in front of you or hold in your hand an object or food of great desire to the student

- place a picture of that item in front the student

- demonstrate in some way to the student how he can hand you that picture to receive the item

- once the student understands he can exchange the picture for the item, he has developed a powerful skill to get what he wants

- work to generalize this skill into making requests for other options in other situations

The Picture Exchange Communication System (PECS) details a sequence of teaching a student to make a request.[2] This system works particularly well with students who have not mastered the skill of initiating communication. It teaches them to clearly demonstrate communicative intent.

Some students do not understand the power of selection in making a choice. They perceive it more like a labeling activity. This happens occasionally to students who have spent considerable time learning how to label pictures or objects as a language development activity. When they see the choices, they label the items, not realizing it means they are selecting and will get what they are labeling. Therefore, what they say may not actually be what they want. They do not seem to understand the difference between the function of labeling and the function of requesting. In addition, they may not realize the rejection nature of making a choice. Choosing one thing means rejecting the other options.

Whichever variation you use to teach making requests or choices, remember that it is critical to:

- use this as an opportunity to teach and reinforce communicative intent

- encourage eye contact and body orientation to you

- discourage grabbing. . . grabbing is not an acceptable skill in the long-term picture

What else can students choose besides food?

It is most common to allow students to choose food items. Remember that there can be dozens and dozens of opportunities to make choices throughout the day. Have students choose:

- which clothing to wear
- which book to read
- which CD to listen to
- which video to watch
- which restaurant to go to
- which seat to sit in
- which person to walk with
  - which cereal to buy
  - which washcloth to use
  - which computer program to use
  - which food to cook
  - which job to do
- AND LOTS MORE

COOKING

I want to work with:

☐ Danny

☐ Carrie

☐ Elizabeth

☐ Mike

☐ Emily

☐ Abigail

☐ Lewis

There are endless opportunities to make requests and choices in a student's life. It is very common to begin to teach these skills in activities related to food since food is such a motivator for most students. Once students learn to exercise their power in food related structured settings, there will be opportunities to use that skill in other life situations. Remember that students may not generalize this skill for other needs and desires unless they are *specifically taught* in a variety of situations.

play with the dog   go to Grandma's house   go in the car

Is it really that important to give students choices and allow them to make requests?

Emphatically *yes!* This technique *significantly* affects behavior. Integrating choice making into the student's life teaches communication and avoids behavior problems. When students have good communication skills, they express their choices and preferences without even being asked. When they are less able to communicate, adults forget to offer choices. Instead, the student's wants and needs may be dictated or anticipated so that he does not have much opportunity to control his environment.

This can be observed easily at the school lunch table. Inevitably there will be a student sitting there with a lunch in front of him full of food he never eats. Sitting next to him will be someone eating items that are tantalizingly attractive. The result looks like a behavior problem:

- he keeps trying to take other children's food

- he throws his food

- he won't eat at lunch time and then he perseverates by asking for snacks all afternoon

A more verbal student would have complained to Mom about what she puts in his lunch or he would negotiate a trade with one of his classmates.

> When a student is demonstrating inappropriate behavior or has a fit about something, offering him some alternate choices is an effective way to intervene and stop the problem. Giving him a chance to choose something else helps to stop the inappropriate behavior.

Go out to eat		
McDonald's	Pizza Hut	Kentucky Fried Chicken
El Pollo Loco	Carl's Jr.	Denny's

The EAT-DRINK Controversy

Some students need to begin training at a very basic level. In an attempt to make tasks simpler for those students, some educators decide to make EAT and DRINK the two choices. They believe those choices will be the simplest for a student to make. Consider this: How does a student with limited ability understand the difference between eating and drinking? From the student's point of view, everything goes in his mouth. Differentiating between solid and liquid is a very high level, abstract skill. A much simpler, easier task would be to give choices of very specific items: Do you want juice or a banana?

THE POINT IS: Teaching students to make requests and choices reduces behavior problems by giving them more control over their lives. Making choices helps:

• increase attention

• improve communicative intent

• get student's real wants and desires met

• increase vocabulary

• increase active participation in communication interactions

• decrease behavior difficulties

• distract students when they are having a problem

Remember that making these opportunities very *visual* will help the students to participate more successfully.

TEACHING PROTEST AND REJECTION SKILLS

Protest is not a bad thing. We want students to be able to tell us what they don't want just as effectively as how they tell us what they do want. Knowing how to communicate protest in a socially acceptable manner is a critically important skill. It is equally important for students to understand and know how to respond to the protest strategies of other people. Difficulty with either expressing or understanding protest frequently results in inappropriate behavior.

Remember that you need to teach the student:

- *how to understand* the protest techniques of other people

- *how to respond* when someone protests

- *how to use* protest strategies that will effectively get their needs met

It will probably work best to intermingle the teaching of these skills. The more students realize how they can use protest skills, the more they will understand when and how others protest.

Do you mean we are supposed to teach students how to protest? Don't they do enough of that already?

Many people don't even consider teaching students to protest because they are afraid that the students will get out of control. In reality, the adults may fear losing their own control. It is important to remember that *students already protest.* They express their protest with whatever communication forms have worked for them in the past. That means they frequently use what we consider bad or inappropriate behavior. The goal is to teach them some options that are more socially appropriate and that will more effectively accomplish what they desire. Remember that students who have better communication skills communicate protest as a natural part of what they do.

> *It is very easy to associate protest with anger or inappropriate behavior because protest is frequently communicated in an angry style. Perhaps protest turns to anger so frequently because the student's other communication attempts don't work as well. The question: How often do students use more acceptable forms of rejecting that are not honored or respected by others? How often do they resort to the more angry, aggressive forms of protest because those are the forms that work for them?*

> *One of the most common causes of unsuccessful teaching is trying to teach too much all at the same time. Students become confused. It can seem laborious to teach one thing at a time, but matching the speed of teaching to the student's speed of learning will produce long term success. One of the most frequent complaints is that students do things inconsistently. Perhaps that occurs because they have not thoroughly learned each skill.*

What do you recommend teaching? What is a proper protest technique to teach?

The answer to this question may not be simple. Selecting *what* to teach will depend on:

- **The student's age:** Young children use different language and forms of communication than teenagers.

- **Overall language ability:** Students who are just emerging in developing language usually benefit from learning at least one generic protest as part of their early vocabulary. It gives them power. Students who have developed more communication skills can learn a greater variety of things to say or do.

- **Long term learning capacity:** If the student learns very slowly and has the long term potential for a ten word vocabulary, you have to select one or two generic choices that will yield him the most for his effort. For students with the potential for learning more language, the number of words to teach will depend on their speed of learning and their social needs.

- **Speed of learning:** Although some students are capable of learning several items simultaneously, students who learn more slowly generally make more progress if you teach one phrase or response repeatedly until it is learned with some spontaneity before adding another one to their menu of choices. Because you are teaching one skill at a time, try to select the most generic, universal choices to begin.

- **What the student's peer group says or does:** It is common for adults to teach students adult language rather that student language. Students need to learn strategies that are typical for their peers.

- **The student's overall social ability:** Students who *appear* to have more social skills can have the most difficulty because they are expected to understand what they are saying. They try to manage social situations by imitating what they see others do. In reality they may blunder by using the wrong phrases or actions with the wrong people or in the wrong situations.

- **The student's ability to discriminate appropriate Vs inappropriate:** Some students can learn the social rules better than others can. Even though it may be acceptable to tell a peer to "bug off", if a student said that to a teacher, he might end up in the principal's office. Teaching appropriate use is a necessary part of the training. If the student isn't capable of making independent decisions about appropriateness, it is probably better to teach him "safe" vocabulary.

- **What the student *needs* to communicate:** Observing the student's social interactions with others will reveal where the frustrations occur. When a difficulty arises, think about what vocabulary or actions other students might use. Those will be the words and actions to teach. Teaching to the situation helps, however, the most progress will be made when addressing frequently occurring needs.

What kinds of protest strategies do you recommend teaching?

Think of both non-verbal and verbal forms of communication. The most effective communication attempts will combine both. The best answer to this question will come from watching the student's peer group.

> ***Typical non-verbal protest strategies include:***
> - Shaking your head "no"
> - Gently pushing something or someone away
> - Holding up your hand to mean "stop"
> - Using gestures
> - Moving away
> - Giving an object back to someone
> - Facial grimaces

Verbal Protests and Responses:

There are multitudes of verbal options. The following list was compiled from interviewing several students ranging in age from preschool through high school. Typical verbal protests range from polite to "kid culture vocabulary". Students communicate protest in part by the intonation that they use to express it. That is what makes the phrases difficult to use or to understand.

What can you say when someone is bothering you or when you don't want something?

I want to be left alone	Don't do that
No	I don't care
No thank you	Shit! Damn it! . . .Etc.
I don't want it	Nonsense!
Please don't do that	You are so silly!
Mine!	Imagine that!
You're a jerk	Whatever!
You idiot	What's that . . . ?
Dork!	You don't have a clue
You're stupid!	Give me a break
Go away	You've got to be kidding me
Leave me alone!	I'll do it some other time
You're annoying me.	Bug off
You're bothering me	Get away
You're making me mad	Get over it
Get outta here	I'm sorry
Mind your own business	Knock it off
I don't want to	Butt head
Get a life	Who died and made you boss?
Not right now	Enough already!
Whatever	Gag me with a spoon
Stay away from me	Gag me with a ginsa
You don't know what you are talking about	
Other unprintable vocabulary	

Words that have a different meaning with negative intonation:

Yah, right!	Come on.. . .
Love it	*Not*
Fine!	

Now, after looking at that list, how do you choose what vocabulary to teach a student who has difficulty with communication? You could probably add many words to the list by enlisting the aid of some students. It is critical to focus the teaching on both understanding and use. What do others mean when they use these words? Which words should you say or communicate to others?

Some of that vocabulary is not very desirable!

Bug off, butt head! Recognize that student language is not adult language. This is an area of teaching that is particularly important because deciding *what* to teach students can make a huge difference in how they are able to handle their social environments. Adults frequently teach students nice polite proper language. That is not what their peers use. If they sound too adult and proper when they speak, they seem socially different from their peers. If the other students use the "kid culture vocabulary," our special student may not have a clue what they are talking about.

Won't people think the students are demonstrating bad behavior if they use some of that language?

Yes, that could cause a problem. They may also encounter difficulty if they already use some of that language but use it with the wrong people or at the wrong time. Because of their difficulty with social judgement, there is a huge potential for problems. That is why we need to teach appropriate skills.

Helping Students Understand:

- Teach students what these phrases mean when other people use them. When they recognize these phrases in other people's communication they will be able to respond more appropriately.

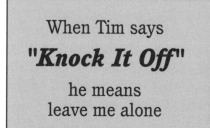

When Tim says

"*Knock It Off*"

he means
leave me alone

- Help students recognize that intonation makes a big difference in the meaning of many phrases. For example: The word *fine* can mean something is wonderful. It can also mean, "If that's the way you want it . . . .see if I care." Intonation of the voice will make the difference.

- Sometimes these words are used in playful social interaction. Someone is attempting to be funny. Sometimes they are used in anger. It can be difficult to discriminate the difference.

- Emphasize that watching a person's body language and facial expressions can change the meaning of these words and help you understand that person better.

Say: **I Don't Know**

Remember that difficulty with these types of skills is at the heart of communication impairment in autism spectrum disorders and in many students with learning disabilities, emotional impairment and other moderate to severe communication disorders. By definition, these students have difficulty with social skills and social judgement. They will not learn these types of skills easily. They may or may not learn appropriate skills by imitation. The problem is that they frequently imitate the wrong things. . . .the undesirable communication behaviors that attract a lot of attention. That means we need to make sure to teach them ways to handle situations appropriately. We need to specifically teach appropriate skills.

Helping students express themselves:

- Teach students to use phrases that will work for a variety of situations. If a student only has the capacity to learn a select few phrases on the list, choose powerful ones.

- Teach students several options. Help them select an appropriate phrase from their menu of choices. Learning to evaluate a situation and make a choice that will be effective for a situation is invaluable.

- Teach that there is a difference between talking to adults and talking to other students. There are some things that are ` appropriate to say to people in authority and there are other things that will get them into trouble.

- Help students understand that there are *degrees* of protest. What you would say to stop a minor annoyance may be very different from handling something that is a major disturbance. There is a difference between being a little bit mad and very very mad.

VISUAL TECHNIQUES FOR TEACHING REJECTION AND PROTEST

• Demonstrate
Model how to protest or reject. Take advantage of the opportunities that occur naturally throughout the day. Exaggerate your expression and your gestures. Repeat what you do more than once. Encourage the student to imitate you. Set up situations where there are multiple opportunities to reject or protest in a short period of time. Frequent repetition will yield a faster learning curve than occasional incidents.

• Use visual tools
Teach the student how to understand and what to say with visual tools. Visual prompts provide the structure for learning specific skills.

• **Try role playing**

Demonstrate appropriate and inappropriate protest and rejection behaviors. Give the students the opportunity to practice the behavior and vocabulary. Make the interactions as realistic as possible so the students will be able to generalize to real life occurrences.

• **Practice in front of a mirror**

Encourage the student to watch you in the mirror while you demonstrate. Then have him practice the same skill, watching himself in the mirror.

• **Use a video camera**

Tape events or practice sessions. Then watch the video tape over and over again. The actions may occur too quickly for the students to really absorb and understand the social exchanges. They cannot process the information rapidly enough. Watching the tapes of correct behavior can help them remember the routine. Combine watching the video with actual practice.

• **Try Instant Replay**

When the student is involved in a real life situation that is not handled properly, stop everything and teach to the situation at that time. Give the student the information he needs . . . either how to understand the situation or how to communicate in that situation. Then let that event occur again. It may be helpful to inform the other students what instant replay is and why you are using it. That way they will be more cooperative in handling it the way you need to really teach what needs to be taught at that moment.

• **Watch TV**

Try taping a soap opera or similar "emotional drama". Watch the video without the sound on. Talk about how the actors look. . . what emotion they are expressing. Don't just watch a whole show. Identify a few good visual examples of what you are teaching and watch those examples over and over.

• **Write it down**

When there is a problem, write about the situation like a story to help the student recall the event and think about what happened. Describe what happened and what should have happened. Explain whatever the student doesn't understand. Writing this information down supports better recall than verbal conversation.

> *Prompting strategies work very well if you can use two people to teach the skill. One person is the communication partner and the other person prompts the student to produce the correct response. Although teaching with two people is frequently ideal, it is often not a possibility. If you are by yourself, you do what you can with what you have to work with. Just be aware of the two-person strategy and utilize it when you have the opportunity.*

When someone sits in your chair

Say: "move please".

SAMPLES & EXAMPLES

PROBLEM: Alex is emerging in his ability to let people know what he wants. When it is time for a meal or snack he tries to let Mom know what he wants to eat. Sometimes she has difficulty understanding what he is trying to choose. If she pulls the wrong item out of the cupboard, Alex screams and cries and pokes his eye.

CAUSE: Alex knows how to use screaming and crying and poking his eye as forms of protest. He hasn't yet learned any more appropriate strategies to communicate that message. When children are learning to make choices, life does not become instantly perfect for them. Sometimes what they really want is not offered as one of the options. Sometimes their choice making skills are not clear yet or they choose something that is not really their choice. They don't know how to "undo" a mistake or they don't know how to let you know they changed their mind. There are times when the adult does not understand and offers the wrong item.

SOLUTION: Teach Alex some more appropriate ways to communicate no. Shaking his head no, pushing the item away, and vocalizing NO! are all skills that would be useful in this situation.

To teach these skills most effectively it is desirable to show Alex what to do before he uses his inappropriate protest behaviors. It may help to set-up the situation a bit so you have the opportunity to jump in and teach the skill before the negative behavior begins. Watch for an opportunity when you know the correct item for sure. Begin to offer the wrong one and immediately prompt Alex to communicate no. Physically prompt him to use his hand to gently push it away. Help him shake his head or vocalize no. It may be a temptation to set-up every interaction this way. Avoid that! If you do it too often you will have a really confused kid. Although this is an excellent teaching strategy, too much of a good thing is not better.

PROBLEM: Allen is very skilled at building intricate structures with the blocks in the classroom. He plays alone and resents intrusion from other students. If another student approaches or touches his blocks, he hits them. Of course, this is not an acceptable way for him to communicate with his peers.

CAUSE: Allen's autism has a lot to do with this situation. He is possessive about his toys and does not want people in his space. He does not have good language skills for manipulating the situation.

SOLUTION: Allen needs to learn better social skills. His teacher decided he would benefit from learning to tolerate other students playing closer to him. Teaching him to say, *"please don't touch"* helped the situation. She made a picture card to remind him to use the language. She also taught him to hold out his hand to gesture to keep away. Using the words and gesture alerted the other students to respect Allen's construction. Once he was assured they were not going to disturb his work, he tolerated them playing closer or with the same materials.

> Things to say when someone is bothering your toys.
>
> I want to do it myself.
>
> I don't want help.
>
> Please don't touch it.

NOTE: Teaching the polite words such as *please* and *thank you* needs careful consideration. Students with autism do not learn language in the same way that other students do. It is important to remember that students like Allen tend to learn language in chunks and phrases. For Allen, *"please don't touch"* is like one word. He will probably learn it as one big piece. For this situation the teacher decided to add the word *"please"* because *"don't touch"* tends to sound harsh and bossy. In an attempt to teach good manners, some people try to teach polite words with everything the students say. Frequently the students do not even understand what the words mean. The result is rote memorization of longer and longer phrases to get their ideas across. It is not advisable to add those polite words on everything, however, watch for situations where they will help a student appear more appropriate.

NO HITTING

Say: Please don't do that

When someone is bothering you...

no pinching

no hitting others

When someone is bothering you...

Say   Leave me alone

Say   You are making me mad

Say   You are bothering me

PROBLEM: Eddie was standing in line at the door. Another student bumped into Eddie. Eddie turned around and attacked the student. It was not a pretty picture!

CAUSE: The other student tripped and bumped into Eddie. It was an accident. . .a typical school situation. Eddie's perception was that he was being attacked. His aggressive attack was so strong because he was defending himself. Even tough Eddie can talk, he doesn't know how to use language to handle challenging or emotional situations.

SOLUTION: Eddie needs to learn some language to manage difficult situations. Teaching him some generic phrases that work for a lot of situations will give him the ability to use language rather than behavior to handle problems.

PROBLEM: Micah is playing with the other students more and more. His use of language is increasing. He is beginning to imitate some of the language the other students use that is not very proper or appropriate. For example: Micah was busy finishing his favorite video game. When the teacher called his name, Micah responded by saying, *"Get outta here dork!"* He really caused a commotion when he told the principal, *"Leave me alone, damn it!"*

CAUSE: Micah is imitating the language used by his peers, however, he doesn't understand the social rules that the other students do. They realize that talking to adults is different from talking to other students and they use different language accordingly. Micah needs to learn more discernment about what to say and when.

SOLUTION: Solving these problems may take a bit of extra thinking. There are several factors to consider. Devising the solution depends a lot on how much Micah understands and how much social understanding he is capable of learning.

The first inclination may be to attempt to teach him a list of words that he *cannot* say. The only problem with this approach is that:

- the list may grow to mammoth proportions

- focusing on the things you do not want him to say may encourage him to say them even more frequently to get a reaction from you

- it may be difficult to give Micah a different set of rules from the rest of the students

- Micah may get confused or angry when other students are breaking his rules

But. . . .it may work. If you tell him not to do it, it may work. That depends on Micah. But, there may be some other strategies that will work better.

Consider these other options:

- Sometimes ignoring words or behaviors is the best thing if you think they will not reoccur.

- Immediately correct him or model what he should say in that situation.

- If you decide it is important to address the situation, very clearly communicate to Micah what he did that was not right and how to correct it. Make it a visual conversation.

- Focus on the positive. Teach Micah proper ways to talk to adults. Teach him what he *can* say.

- Begin to teach the concept of good manners and bad manners.

> *It is very easy for us to tell students what they are doing that is wrong. We tell them to stop or we punish them. It is easy to forget to communicate very clearly to the student what he **should** do.*

Remember that in devising solutions to these kinds of problems we need to have two goals:

- solve the immediate problem

- teach long term self-management skills

WORDS I CAN USE

Words I can use with adults	*Words I can use with kids*
Please don't do that No thank you Excuse me Yes, Mr. Jenkins	Knock it off Quit that Look out You're a dork!

THE POINT IS: Inappropriate behavior frequently occurs because students have difficulty expressing or understanding protest adequately.

- Students need to be *specifically taught* to understand and use protest and rejection skills

- Because of their disability these skills may be very difficult for students to learn

These teaching strategies work for teaching other social skills, too, however, protest is a good place to begin. Difficulty understanding or using appropriate protest is one of the most common communication-behavior problems.

NOTE: It is *critical* to remember that the solutions you choose need to match the student's level of development and level of understanding.

TEACHING NEGOTIATION LANGUAGE

Students who possess effective communication skills are able to negotiate their options. They are able to manipulate circumstances to achieve a desirable outcome. Students who have communication difficulties are unable to do that.

Is it important for students to be able to negotiate?

This is a very important skill because behavior situations often arise from difficulty in handling these situations. Think about it. It is not unusual for adults to dominate social interactions and dictate the outcomes for students who have less communication ability. Adults have a tendency to try to control students. This is not to suggest that they abdicate their leadership role. But think about the rigidity that can easily dominate a setting. In the name of "structure" we can forget to allow for human error or human-ness.

Since we are talking about behavior, how is this related to behavior?

Behavior is frequently affected by the lack of ability in this area. At one extreme, students become passive because they are helpless to communicate. At the other extreme, students act out because that is the only strategy they know to try to manage the situation.

Our targeted students frequently don't know how to say or effectively communicate concepts that clarify life. Think about the language necessary to negotiate these choice concepts:

- I want both choices.
- I changed my mind.
- I don't know.
- I want a different choice.
- Can I choose something different?
- Can I do something different?

- What are my choices?
- I made a mistake.
- This is not what I thought.
- I don't want either choice.
- I don't know what I want.
- Can I wait until later?

These same students frequently experience difficulty in general conversational situations. They miss information and their thinking and processing machines work more slowly than those of other people do. Our teaching and communication happens at a rapid pace. . . too rapid for some of them to keep up. Simple phrases can help them get the information they need. When students have the ability to control the situation to meet their needs their participation improves significantly. Consider these phrases:

- I don't understand.
- Wait a minute.
- Let me think about that a minute.
- I didn't hear you.
- Will you tell me that again?
- I am thinking.
- Will you show me?
- Will you write that down?

SAMPLES & EXAMPLES

PROBLEM: Brent pointed to the apple on the counter to make a request. After he got the apple in his hand the teacher took out a box of cookies from the cupboard. Brent immediately began a huge tantrum.

CAUSE: There were other choices that Brent was not aware of. After he realized the cookies were there, he had no communication skills to change the situation.

SOLUTION: Teach Brent to hand back the apple and point to what he really wants. Ideally, show him how to do this before his tantrum begins. Once he has his outburst, giving him the cookie becomes a reward for the outburst. If he does have his tantrum, do what you can to get him calm before negotiating the exchange. Sometimes students try in some way to negotiate this exchange but the adult ignores the negotiation. Or perhaps the adult has the attitude that the student already made a choice and he shouldn't get another one. Rather than get stuck in the discipline of the situation, look at it as an opportunity to teach a communication skill.

> *Adults frequently back themselves into win-lose situations. When the student and adult are in conflict, one wins and one loses. Rather than get stuck in the discipline of the situation, look at it as an opportunity to teach a communication skill.*

PROBLEM: Todd has a hard time paying attention when others are talking. Frequently, by the time he realizes the teacher is talking to him, he has missed the first part of the question or direction. He blurts out answers even when he didn't hear the entire question.

CAUSE: Todd's diagnosis of attention deficit disorder is a major part of his problem.

SOLUTION: Todd benefits from people communicating to him using visual tools. The visual tools help get his attention and help him focus on what they are saying. Unfortunately, all of life cannot be visual. During those situations where no visual support is available, Todd needs to learn to ask for support. Telling a person, "I didn't hear you," or "Will you write that down?" can help Todd cope with difficult circumstances. The challenge: Todd needs to realize he has a problem before he will remember to ask for help. He may need to learn to recognize when he has a problem.

Negotiation can occur non-verbally as well as verbally, although it will occur most frequently with verbal language. All students will not learn this language. This vocabulary is probably too difficult or confusing for students who are just learning choice making or those who are emerging in developing language skills. These types of phrases are appropriate for those students who have reached a level of conversational language.

THE POINT IS: Students benefit from learning negotiation language. Teaching these types of phrases:

- gives them skills to manage difficult situations

- prevents them from using less desirable behaviors

- teaches them to get all the information they need before responding

- helps them participate more appropriately

What can you say when you don't understand?

1. Please say that again.

2. I didn't hear you.

3. I don't know what you are talking about.

4. I don't understand.

5. What?

6. What did you say?

7. I don't comprehend.

8. Huh?

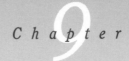

C h a p t e r

9

Using Visual Tools To Regulate Behavior

It is common to talk about providing a *structured environment* for students.

What is structure? What does it take for students to be comfortable in an environment?

Structure refers to the things we do to make the environment predictable for students. When students know what to expect and how to behave, they are more relaxed. . .more content. *They like it when we give them lots of information because they don't have to spend so much energy trying to figure life out.* Visual tools help the students manage their behavior by clarifying some of the difficult-to-understand abstractness of life. Giving them information is critical. We need to clearly let them know what is or what is not acceptable. Rules help by telling them how to act. Using concrete ways to help them understand abstract concepts guides them to better behavior.

Isn't it being too strict to give them a lot of rules to follow?

On the contrary, rules provide a welcome structure to life. *It is much easier to participate if you know exactly what is expected from you.* When you have to guess all the time, life is frustrating. It also gets really really frustrating when you don't completely understand some of those abstract things that dictate how we are supposed to behave. What we call behavior problems is frequently students behaving in certain ways because they don't understand the social rules. They do not clearly understand what they should or should not do. When they do understand, they may have difficulty managing themselves appropriately. They have a lot to think about. Visual tools help. Let's explore this more.

COMMUNICATING NO

- *"No, you can't have it."*

- *"No, don't do that"*

- *"No, there isn't any more milk."*

- *"No, we aren't going to the dentist, we are going to the ice cream store instead."*

- *"I know what. . .let's play your favorite game!"*

I didn't think NO was so hard to understand, but I can see already where the problems begin!

Can you understand the confusion? In the context of giving information, *no* is a powerful word. Parents begin using it with very young children to correct them. In normal development, it is generally one of the first words children learn to understand. Students with autism spectrum disorders, other communication difficulties and behavior problems have heard more than their share of this word. The way the concepts are communicated can significantly affect how they will respond.

The word NO really has a lot of different meanings, doesn't it?

No is used to convey a wide variety of concepts. Imagine the child who frequently hears *no* meaning "Don't do what you are doing, you are being bad." He develops a pattern of reacting to that word. Then when he is told "*No*, there isn't any more," he may respond as if he were told "*No* – you were bad and you can't have any." It gets confusing, doesn't it? We are dealing with students who have difficulty understanding concepts and relationships. The word *no* can have a zillion different meanings. But the first way they learn that word is probably in the form of a correction for being bad or doing something dangerous. That means the student heard a strong word that may have been followed by some other prompting or corrections to make sure the child understood. The child first learns this word associated with something negative. No wonder he responds strongly when he hears it in different contexts.

HOW TO COMMUNICATE NO

1. Use a variety of terminology
When communicating any of these concepts, terminology is important. Informing a student that "We will do it *later*." may produce a more positive response than saying "No-not now." Telling the student that his favorite snack is *"all gone"* might produce a different response from answering "No you can't have any." Some students benefit from combined phrases such as, "There is *no more*. . . it is *all gone*."

2. Use visual tools
Visual tools assist communicating the concepts in more concrete ways. This is an opportunity to use your creativity. It is important to develop systems that *make sense to students.* The goal is to have activities, choices and other information represented visually so the negation can be shown visually.

3. Give students lots of related information
It is just as important to be able to give them the visual information about what is not available as what is available. They often need to know what not to do in addition to knowing what to do. Let them know when they can do something if it can't be now. Students need to understand that it will happen but at a later time. Tell them the other options when they want the one that is not available.

4. Demonstrate what *NO* means
Just because you tell the student and show him with a symbol what you mean, it doesn't mean he will understand. It may be necessary to prompt him or guide him or use additional means to help him understand exactly what you are trying to communicate.

5. Teach students how to respond to *NO*
If students have a history of bad experiences related to *no,* expect a negative response whenever you use that term. Teach them what else to say or do in those circumstances.

NOTE: There are some people who feel it is inappropriate to use *no* with these students. The word *no* is a valuable and powerful word. Use it. Just don't over-use it. Be aware of how students respond and be ready to modify what you communicate so you can get the student response you desire. Don't eliminate it. Just use it effectively.

TECHNIQUES FOR INDICATING NO

• Use the international *NO* sign

That symbol has a strong appearance that students easily identify. It can be placed on cabinets where students may not go or doors where they may not exit. Place it on rule charts to emphasize unacceptable behaviors.

• Use other symbols to represent some of the *NO* concepts

What is most critical is to use symbols the students understand. Match this to the student's language and communication level. Introducing too much to a student who won't comprehend will not improve communication.

• Cover things up

When something is not available it may seem logical to remove it, i.e. on a choice board. The problem is that the simple removal of the item does not ensure that the student will understand that it is unavailable. The student may perseverate on a request for an item removed from a choice board because he remembers it. Once you remove the picture, it is not available anymore to use for communication purposes. Instead, turn it over or cover it up. Then it is still a useful communication tool.

• Use additional visual tools to explain the concept

Pull something else out of your visual toolbox to help the student understand the situation. Use the tools to tell them when or what else or whatever information will help them understand. Remember, several visual tools often work together to help the students really grasp what we want them to understand.

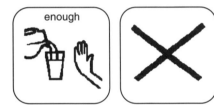

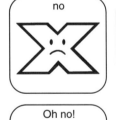

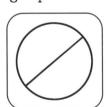

TEACHING STUDENTS TO COMMUNICATE NO

Students do communicate *no*, however, it usually occurs in the context of protest. *No* is the universal word that works in a lot of situations. If they have a limited number ways to communicate protest you will probably see a lot of negative behavior used as a means to attempt to control situations. It is important for students to learn some alternate ways to manage situations. Teaching them some different vocabulary to say or communicate helps them have more control.

Alternate Vocabulary to Consider for Communicating NO

• No	• I don't want to
• Do it later	• No more
• Not now	• That's enough
• I'm not finished	• Stop
• All done	• Don't do it
• I'm finished	• Don't go
• I don't know	• Leave me alone
• I don't like it	• Mine

THE POINT IS: Behavior difficulties easily arise because of the simple word *no*. Either students react because they don't understand the many ways that word is used, or they do not communicate it themselves in an appropriate and effective way.

- *No* is a very powerful word that can cause a lot of misunderstanding.

- Remember that the concept *no* can be communicated with a variety of vocabulary.

- Visual tools help clarify what *no* means

ESTABLISHING RULES AND BEHAVIOR GUIDELINES

Most students do not purposely intend to "be bad." As we have discovered, the behavior that we observe occurs for a variety of reasons. Visual tools help students know how to behave. They help the student know what we expect them to do.

Visual rules are used:

- to tell students what *to* do
- to tell students what *not* to do
- to define consequences (if. . . .then)

Why don't these students know the rules?

They don't understand. They don't remember. Perhaps they have learned different routines and don't know how to change. Our targeted students can perceive their world very differently from the way others understand it. Consider life from the student's perspective.

1. Students may be oblivious to the social frameworks that we use to modify our own behavior. They appear to be "into themselves" or internally driven. This can result in:

- self stimulation
- entertaining themselves without being aware of our requests
- impulsively meeting their own needs without concern for proper behavior or social rules
- difficulty adhering to external constraints on their impulsive attempts at self direction or self gratification

2. Their communication disorder prevents appropriate behavior.

- They don't understand *what* is happening or what is required
- They don't understand *why* they need to follow certain rules
- They may be doing what they *think* they are supposed to do
- They do not realize they are not doing what we want
- They don't understand the contingencies of life
- They may use behavior as a form of communication when they don't have other more effective means to manipulate their environment

3. They do not adequately interpret social information to modify their actions.

- They are not able to accurately interpret the non verbal information that guides behavior choices
- They do not comprehend the social implications of actions and choices

4. They are doing what they have learned and what makes sense to them.

They do not understand that their learned behavior is not appropriate for the situation and they do not know what else to do.

- They are demonstrating *learned behavior*
- They are following *learned routines* but they may not be following the correct routine
- They do not know how to adjust their learned behavior to fit specific situations

Each person can be inconsistent in how they respond to the student's behavior. Inconsistency also occurs between people. One allows a behavior that the other corrects. The result is confusion. Making rules visual helps the adults in charge as much as it helps the students. Then the adults know what rules to enforce.

Don't adults teach the rules?

We certainly try. The typical way is to tell students over and over again what we want. But even if students demonstrate a desire to cooperate and participate, they may not be particularly successful due to our style of handling behavior situations. Very often students do not do what we want because:

1. We do not clearly communicate what we expect

- we use vague, unclear language
- we communicate verbally without supporting that communication with other forms to ensure student understanding
- we are not specific about what we expect
- we talk too much and students can't sort out what we really want

2. We do not expect what we communicate

- we make requests that are not realistic
- we do not follow up to help the student follow through to comply with our request

3. We are inconsistent in our expectations

When the student does not do what we want:

- sometimes we respond to correct him
- sometimes we ignore the lack of compliance
- sometimes we react strongly or in anger

Isn't it hard for students to follow a lot of rules?

Actually, developing rules makes it *easier* for students. Knowing clearly what to do is easier than guessing. The rules clearly communicate how you expect students to participate. They serve as reminders to the students to help them remember what they need to remember. There is something very commanding about visual rules. Things in print carry an authority that has more power than human interaction.

From the student perspective, life is complicated. There are some things that are always OK to do and other actions that are never OK. Housed between those two extremes is a huge "gray area". That center ground is filled with the *"sometimes"* of life. Sometimes you can do it; sometimes you can't. Sometimes you can have it; sometimes not. Sometimes you are corrected or punished; sometimes laughter prevails. It is hard to figure out. Rules make that easier. Either you are following the rules or you are not following them.

Isn't it awkward for the parents and educators to create a lot of rules?

The rules actually help adults manage students better. The rules make it clear what behaviors to pay attention to or correct. They serve as guides to evaluate if students are being successful.

This is what happens to the adults in charge:

- They change their minds.
- They get distracted.
- They get busy with something else.
- They forget what they were requesting.
- They change the rules.

> *When a student has a lot of areas of difficulty it is easy to react and try to correct everything he does. That can cause a constant state of disharmony. Pick your battlegrounds. Choose which behaviors are the most critical ones to deal with. Those are the ones to put in rule form.*

We help students participate more effectively by clearly communicating rules or guidelines that they need to follow. Creating rules reduces the number of judgments they need to make. It is easy for students to follow specific rules. It is harder for them to try to interpret rapidly changing social situations and then figure out what to do to respond.

Truthfully, we are quite inconsistent in our enforcement of rules and expectations. Then we get frustrated and that frustration easily turns to anger. Lack of consistency is human nature. For as much as we talk about students needing consistency, it is extremely difficult to define. Rules help us be dependable. They clarify lots of the gray area.

Developing visual rules provides valuable structure for the adults. The process of developing the rules causes us to think through exactly how we want to handle the problem behavior or situation. It helps us specifically define what is acceptable behavior and what will not be permitted. It helps us think through the process in a logical fashion so we will be able to act purposely and consistently when the behaviors occur. Using the visual rules help us follow through with consistency and avoid strong reactions to situations.

How do you define student success?

From the adult perspective, there are two conditions. . .what is acceptable and what is not acceptable. *Either students are following the rules or they are not.* If students are not following the rules, the visual tools help direct them to modify their behavior.

DEVELOPING GENERAL RULES

A simple place to begin is to establish some basic classroom rules.
These can be general so they apply to everyone. Try to choose general
rules that will apply across a variety of circumstances. For example:

- sit
- be quiet
- listen to the teacher
- be nice to your friends
- do your work

Rules like these can apply nicely to almost every situation that could
arise in the classroom. Most of the common behavior difficulties that
occur in a typical classroom could be corrected by stating one of
these rules.

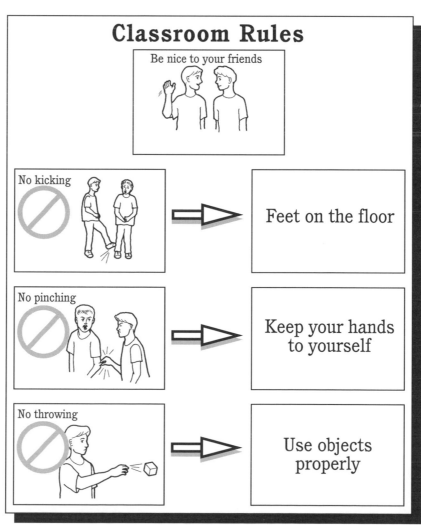

HOW TO USE RULES

1. Post the rules visually
Put them in a location that can be easily viewed. Make sure they are large enough for students to see from far away.

2. Review the rules on a regular basis
Start the day by reviewing the rules. Have the students look at the rules; point to them, label them or whatever system you design to get them actively involved. Go back to review the rules as often as necessary to keep them fresh in the student's thinking. For some students, reviewing the rules in the morning is enough. Other students may need to be reminded at the beginning of each new activity throughout the day.

3. Use the visual rules
When the student's behavior needs correcting, communicate the correct behavior by showing the rule and stating what the student needs to do.

4. Wait expectantly
Pause to give the student the time necessary to modify his behavior to match the direction.

5. Prompt as needed
If the rule is unfamiliar or there is some question about the student's comprehension of the rule, support your direction with the necessary level of prompting to guide his accomplishment of the request.

6. Restate the rule as needed and wait for compliance

7. Decide what to do next
If the student does not follow the rule, it will be necessary to decide if further waiting is appropriate. There may be a point when the student requires some form of prompting or guidance to accomplish the directive. What to do at this stage will depend on the student, on the student's current behavior and on your knowledge of the student. Past experience will help guide this decision.

CLASSROOM RULES

 Be quiet

 Listen to the teacher

 Do your work

 Play nice with your friends

Use visual rules to redirect a student when there is a problem.
When a difficulty arises or the student's behavior needs
correcting, *show* him the rule and *tell* him what he needs to do:

• State the script on the rule: *"sit, "be quiet"*, etc.

• Or say: *"The rule is ____"*

• In some extreme cases (depending on the individual student or
circumstance) it may be helpful to *show* the rule and *eliminate
the verbal direction.* This strategy is sometimes effective when
students are very upset or experiencing sensory overload.

INDIVIDUAL RULES

After establishing some general classroom rules, a next step can be to
target individual rules for specific problems. This may not be
necessary for everyone. Depending on need, a student may have one or
more individual rules that target very specific behaviors that need
correction.

What types of behaviors do you target for individual rules?

Think of those reoccurring behaviors or actions that you need to
correct repeatedly. They don't have to be "bad" behaviors. Sometimes
students just need a lot of reminding to acquire appropriate ways of
managing themselves.

Do you make individual rules in the same format as group rules?

Group rules are designed to be very general so they will apply to a
wide variety of possible difficulties. Individual rules are very specific.
Think of a laser that aims at a very specific target.

When determining individual rules it is helpful to state in a positive
way what you want the student to do. At times it is helpful to state
what not to do. Other rules can be stated in both positive and negative
terms to really make a point. It is important to state the rules so they
make sense to the student and help him to modify his behavior.
Consider these. It should be clear what the difficulties are.

SAMPLES & EXAMPLES

PROBLEM: Kenny is a budding teenager whose body functions are working. He has no discreetness about his body needs. He itches and scratches and passes gas and a variety of other things that cause him to be noticed in a negative way by the other students. Since he is developing an adult body, it all looks worse than it did when he was younger.

CAUSE: Kenny's social manners have not developed enough. He is totally unaware of the social implications of some of his behaviors.

SOLUTION: It is important for Kenny to learn what is not socially acceptable. He needs to learn appropriate ways and locations for handling his body needs. Rule cards and cards with additional information will help. In addition, writing some Social Stories® to help Kenny better understand the social environment would help him make better decisions.

Put hands in
pockets

No hands in
your pants

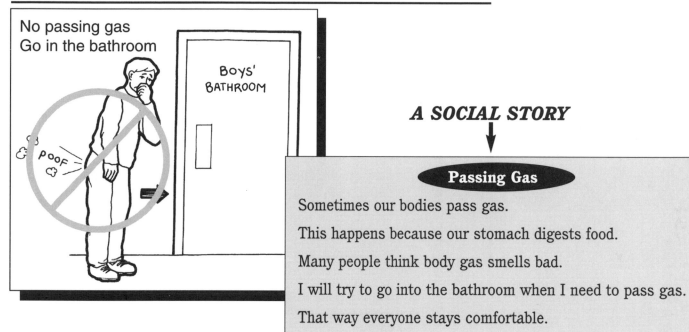

No passing gas
Go in the bathroom

BOYS' BATHROOM

POOF

A SOCIAL STORY

Passing Gas

Sometimes our bodies pass gas.

This happens because our stomach digests food.

Many people think body gas smells bad.

I will try to go into the bathroom when I need to pass gas.

That way everyone stays comfortable.

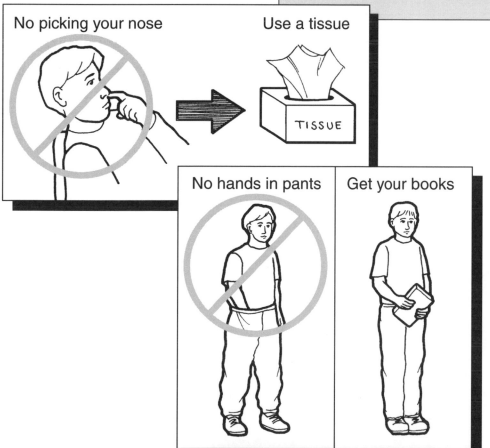

No picking your nose

Use a tissue

TISSUE

No hands in pants

Get your books

Carol Gray has pioneered the writing of Social Stories, which are stories designed to help students know how to handle social situations appropriately. Social Stories are simple stories that are written to describe social situations in a way that helps students understand social cues and social information. They are generally written to address very specific individual problems or needs. Experience with this technique has demonstrated positive changes in student responses to targeted situations in many cases. This is a helpful technique to consider for increasing appropriate behavior and decreasing inappropriate behavior.[3]

Bathroom Rules

Toilet	Go to the bathroom
Toilet Paper	Use toilet paper to wipe
Pants	Fix your pants
Flush	Flush one time
Wash	Wash your hands
Dry	Dry your hands
Go back to the room	

Look at your friends

DESIGNING RULES AND BEHAVIOR GUIDES

How you create a rule chart or behavior guide can determine how well a student will understand it and modify his behavior. Here are some key considerations:

1. Look at the situation from the *student's* point of view

Include the information that makes sense to the student. That may be different from what the adult would normally choose.

2. Be specific

These students don't understand hints or vague suggestions. Tell them exactly what they need to do.

3. Include only the most important information

It is easy to try to include too much. If there is too much, the student will not pay attention or comprehend.

4. Make tools logical and sequential

This is not a time to get overly fancy or artistic. Remember to be logical from the student's viewpoint.

5. Don't be afraid to experiment to see what format or layout works best for the situation

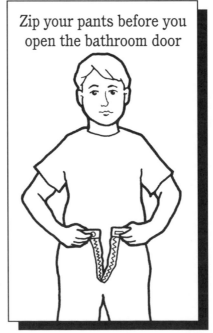

Zip your pants before you open the bathroom door

Sometimes we learn what works best by trial and error. Look at these variations for the same general problems. Which format will work? Sometimes it doesn't matter. For other students one layout may work better than another.

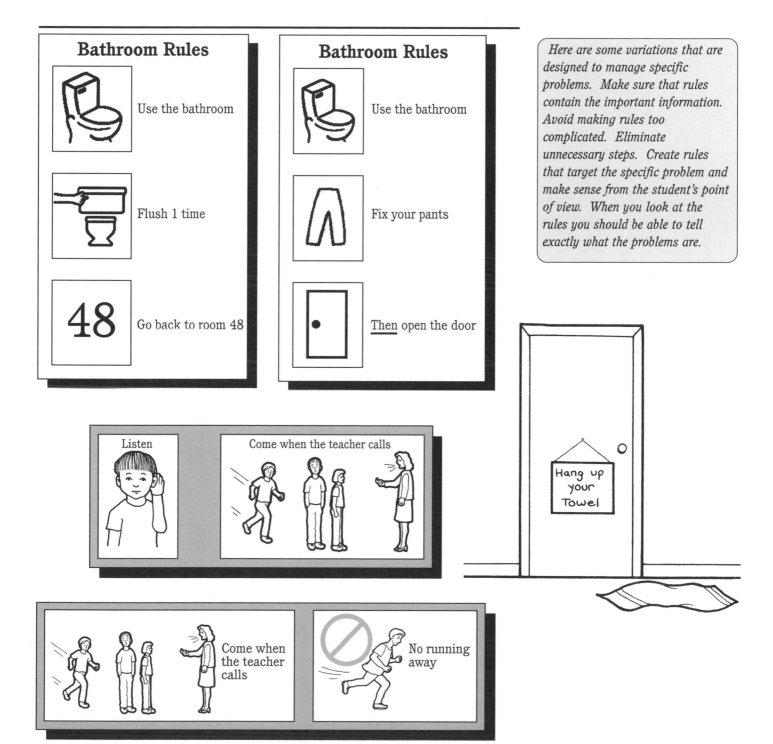

Bathroom Rules

Use the bathroom

Flush 1 time

48 Go back to room 48

Bathroom Rules

Use the bathroom

Fix your pants

<u>Then</u> open the door

Here are some variations that are designed to manage specific problems. Make sure that rules contain the important information. Avoid making rules too complicated. Eliminate unnecessary steps. Create rules that target the specific problem and make sense from the student's point of view. When you look at the rules you should be able to tell exactly what the problems are.

Listen

Come when the teacher calls

Come when the teacher calls

No running away

Hang up your Towel

For most students any one of these layouts would work. Some students may respond to one layout better than the others.

When you ride the bus

Keep your seatbelt on

Do your work

Wear your seatbelt on the bus

LOOKING

Look at your friends when you talk

Look at the teacher

Keep your seatbelt on!!!

Bus

Seatbelt

Do not leave the gym

Listen to the teacher

> *The problem is a student who runs away to search out his favorite books and videos. He disappears quickly when traveling from the classroom to the gym. Which layout will work best to guide him to success? It might be necessary to try more than one option.*

No stopping for videos   No stopping for books   Go to the gym

Stay in the gym

Stay in the gym

No running   Library   Videos

MORE SAMPLES & EXAMPLES

When you observe well designed rule and behavior charts, it should be fairly clear what the problem is. Look at these examples.

Stay with the group

Don't go by yourself

Bobby's Rules

No hitting!

Sit in the chair for 5 minutes

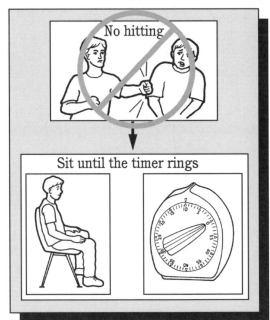

No hitting

Sit until the timer rings

Put the seat up

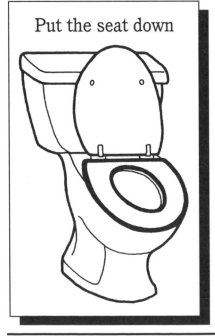

Put the seat down

say HI

HI

Jenny's Rules

 Follow your schedule

 Stay with the group

 Do not eat from the garbage can

 Do not eat the numbers from your book

Work Rules at Buger King

 Wear your uniform

 Do your work

 Finish your work by 2:00

 If you finish your work by 2:00 you can have a snack

Keep your chair in the square

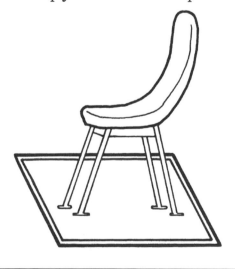

Paul's Rules

 TALK NICE

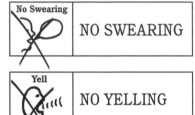 **NO SWEARING**

NO YELLING

 BE NICE TO YOUR FRIENDS

 NO BITING

 NO HITTING

 FOLLOW YOUR SCHEDULE

THE POINT IS:

Visual rules help *students* by:
- defining what to do
- clearly communicating what *not to do*
- reminding students how to handle themselves
- helping students understand what behavior is expected of them

Developing visual rules helps *adults* by:
- clarifying which behaviors are important to attend to
- communicating specifically what the student needs to do
  or not do
- helping adults focusing on correcting selected behaviors rather than attempting to address everything a student does

Chapter 10

Improving Language Skills With Visual Tools

When students begin to develop language, *their behavior can actually appear to get worse before it gets better.* The emergence of language may cause frustration for both the students and their parents or teachers.

What!? Why would developing language cause behavior problems? That doesn't make sense.

One mom stated it this way. She said, "I used to think, 'If only my son could talk, then everything would be OK.' Now that he is talking, I realize the problem is not gone."

She was realizing that just because her son was learning to talk, it didn't mean he could use that language successfully to accomplish what he wanted. That is where the behavior problems explode.

I still don't understand how talking causes behavior problems.

If students are not successful with their attempts to use language, they resort to using the behaviors that they have used successfully in the past. *When the language doesn't work, they will use what does work* (from their point of view).

Many students with autism do not develop verbal language. The exact percentage may be a moving number related to the increasing number of diagnoses of students that are higher skilled. Many behavior problems may be related to the student's ability to communicate. It is important to remember that speech alone does not make a student an effective communicator. A variety of skills combine to create meaningful communication. Effective communication is the primary goal, whether or not a student develops verbal language. For those students who do develop speech, it is imperative to teach the vocabulary that will enhance real social communication.

> *Think of learning language like learning other skills such as operating a computer. Some people just sit down and start punching keys. They seem to automatically know what to do. Other people need help just to find the switch to turn the machine on.*

What we need to remember is that language development is a *process*. Students need to learn lots and lots of words. They also need to learn *how to use* those words. The learning process to do that may be a bumpy road. Typically developing children seem to automatically acquire the words and then instinctively know how to use them for social interaction and to get their wants and needs met. Our targeted population can't do that. They frequently need to be specifically taught exactly what to do and how to do it.

- Some students will need to be taught each individual word they learn.

- Another group of students will need specific training to get their "language machine" started, and once it gets started they will begin to learn more language from the environment.

- There are students who appear to develop vocabulary in a style that is more like typically developing students, however, there will be observable differences in what they know and in how they use that language.

Students in all of these groups will probably need help learning how to use language instead of less desirable behaviors. They will need to learn to select the appropriate language for the situations in their lives. Knowing what language skills to teach will make a difference in how their behavior problems are modified. Let's investigate this further.

DEVELOPING EMERGING LANGUAGE SKILLS

When students are emerging in developing language, it can be challenging to decide what words to teach them. Watching their behavior helps us identify situations where they will benefit from learning more language. The goal is to choose language that will make sense to the students and teach them the power of interacting with others.

I am looking for a good language curriculum to follow for my students.

Evaluate very carefully. Many curriculums are very speech and language oriented. Language curriculums frequently list vocabulary to teach that is academically oriented. It is not unusual for training programs to begin by teaching colors, numbers, farm animals and other typical preschool vocabulary. Although those are nice words to learn, they don't help students manipulate their environments to get their wants and needs met. They don't teach the communication skills necessary to replace behaviors that the students are using. Consequently, students continue to use their collection of inappropriate behaviors to try to control people and the environment. Teaching them a greater variety of acceptable and effective ways to accomplish these same goals is an important place to begin. The vocabulary in those curriculums may not help do that.

Labeling pictures is a common early language learning activity. When children are developing language we tend to spend lots of time with them labeling objects and pictures in storybooks. As the children learn new words, they are then able to use that vocabulary for a variety of purposes (functions). For example: After learning the word *shoe,* they eventually develop the ability to use that word to make a request ("Please tie my shoe.") or ask a question ("Where is my shoe?") or make a comment ("Look at that funny shoe!") or communicate a protest ("I don't want to wear my shoe!")

This same teaching technique is frequently used with students who have communication impairments. But there is a difference in how some of these students learn, particularly those with autism spectrum disorders. After learning to label the pictures, they don't easily generalize to be able to use those words for different functions or purposes. For example, they may be able to label a picture of a banana or a video, but they may not be able to use those words to ask you for the items. Even if they can label a picture of a shoe, that does not mean they can ask you to tie their shoes. *These students seem to learn language better if they learn the vocabulary in the context of real meaningful situations. Rather than just labeling pictures, they learn to use the words better if they are learned in real communication exchanges. Try to capture the moment and teach the language when the students have a real life need.*

Choose words that:

- help the students get their wants and needs met
- enable students to exercise some control over their environment
- give *strong* social response
- help students participate in life routines and activities

Pick words that can occur frequently so students can practice them over and over. When students have many opportunities to use words, they will learn them more quickly. They will use words that have power and meaning to them.

SELECTING VOCABULARY TO TEACH

Can you be more specific? What kind of vocabulary do you recommend teaching?

Begin to think of the categories of needs the students have. Think about what they try to communicate with their behavior. Students frequently encounter difficulty getting their needs met. The majority of their communication attempts are probably requests or protests.

These are some suggestions to teach powerful early communication. They are not listed in any significant order. There could be many word choices that communicate these ideas. Consider teaching communications that convey these needs. These may not be the exact words the student will use, but they are *concepts* he may need to convey.

Requests:

- pay attention to me/look at me
- request food
- request objects/toys/people/activities
- I want _____
- help
- bathroom/potty
- I want to do _____

Protests:

- No
- I don't want it
- leave me alone/go away
- I need to escape/leave
- mine

> *If you are concerned about a student's behavior and he doesn't have some effective language skills for getting his wants and needs met, please don't use his time teaching him to label zoo animals!!!*

Social Interaction:

- HI/BYE
- look at this
- look at that
- oh-oh
- oh-no
- I'm finished/all done
- all gone
- my turn/your turn
- let's play
- I love you

Vocabulary Related to Life and School Routines

- schedule words
- locations we go
- people in my life
- words to songs and activities
- my favorite objects/activities
- what I want
- how I feel

Improving Language Skills with Visual Tools

MORE THOUGHTS ON SELECTING VOCABULARY

Those are great words for young children. What about older students or those who talk more?

First of all, don't be deceived because students talk more. Even though a lot of words or sentences come out of their mouths, it doesn't mean they can really communicate those types of concepts and words. Make sure they can effectively communicate those types of needs. Then, when building more vocabulary, make it personal for the student. Move in this direction:

- *Focus on vocabulary that will replace unacceptable behaviors.*

- Build the student's vocabulary around his life routines.

- Teach the words that will help him communicate his wants and needs.

- Teach communication skills that will help him participate more effectively in social interactions.

- Teach vocabulary that targets what the student is interested in.

> *Food for thought: If a student will only learn to communicate ten things, what should those things be?*

The critical part about selecting vocabulary is to remember the big picture. That will create the need to prioritize. People frequently begin to expand a child's vocabulary by teaching words that:

- have no functional purpose for social interaction

- occur infrequently in the child's life

- are too specific or too generic to be useful

Is there anything else we need to consider when teaching vocabulary?

Yes, there is one more critical point that is highly related to the behavior issues we are concerned about. As students continue to develop language and use it to communicate their wants and needs, we assume that the words they are speaking are communicating what they really intend. This is where a caution light should flash. *Don't just assume that the words that come out of their mouths are the right words for what they are trying to communicate.* This is a crucial point.

Many of these students experience word retrieval problems or memory problems and mental organization difficulties. Sometimes they use memorized echolalic chunks of language that are not specific enough for what they really want to communicate. Their experience can be like reaching into the sock drawer with your eyes closed. You pull out some socks that you can wear, but they may not be the color or style you wanted. In the same way, students can get to the point where they can pull out words when it is their turn to say something, but they may not be very accurate in finding the most appropriate words. Fortunately, this tends to get better with practice.

These students may really crash when they are frustrated or upset or when things are not going their way. Ironically, a few students suddenly become very verbal and use unusually fluent language when angry or severely stressed. Many others experience severe difficulty thinking and sorting through to get the words they need during those stressful times.

- They probably experience more difficulty when there are time pressures for them to perform.

- The words that they know or are able to say may not be what they really want.

- They say words that do not communicate what they really mean.

- They might request a familiar item when that is not what they really want and then they get more upset because they are not getting what they want.

In those challenging times their vocabulary choices are not adequate for their needs. Their apparent intent does not match their real intent. You can imagine what problems can result from this.

How do you help students become more accurate as they develop language skills?

First you have to recognize the problem when it occurs. Learn to listen better. Here is how:

1. Recognize that the words the student uses may not fully represent what he means.

2. Listen not only to the words spoken by the student, but also to the meaning underlying those words. Pay attention to the context of the situation.

3. Observe the student's non-verbal communication to help interpret what his intent is.

Focus on teaching communication, not just speech. Teach him to support his communication attempts visually. The visual supports will help the organization in his brain so he can become more accurate in his speech and clarify what he is intending to communicate.

TEACH COMMUNICATION...
NOT "JUST SPEECH"

Focus on teaching *communication*, not just speech. Remember to *teach the student to use a combination of forms to get his idea across.* Teaching students how to use an effective gesture system to support their communication attempts helps them become more interactive and accomplish their intents better. When teaching students *what* to communicate, remember to teach combinations of skills. Even if they can talk, stress using various non-verbal strategies to support their communication. That means:

1. Using a picture to support what he is communicating

2. Using a gesture to push something away or shaking your head while vocalizing "no"

3. Holding up an object while requesting "help"

4. Pointing or writing down a word while making a request

5. Walking up to a person and taking their hand to pull them to the area where a request needs to be made

6. Using a variety of gestures

7. Using body language

8. Establishing proximity to a person (getting closer to the person)

9. Moving away from a person

10. Pointing

11. Showing objects or actions

12. Showing pictures

13. Using written language to help share information

SAMPLES & EXAMPLES

PROBLEMS: Byron wants desperately to open his own thermos. Sometimes he can and sometimes it won't open. When he has problems he immediately screeches and flails his body around.

Samantha is learning to use the bathroom but she has difficulty managing the zipper and snap on her jeans. She comes back to the classroom with her pants around her knees.

When another student goes near Donny's favorite video game he hits him.

During work time Joe asks to go get a drink many times. He doesn't seem to really want the water. He just stands by the water fountain for a long time and wanders in the hall.

Whenever someone asks Matt, "What do you want?" he always answers "juice". If you try to give him the juice, he cries. Then when he sees the options he makes a different selection.

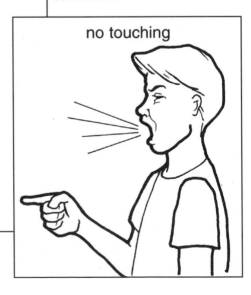

Developing Emerging Language

CAUSE: These students do not know or cannot use adequate vocabulary words to help them manage their concerns.

SOLUTION: Teach them power words to help the situations. Byron needs to ask for help. Samantha needs help, too. If Donny could tell the other person to stay away from his video game he would not feel so threatened. Perhaps Joe needs a way to ask to stop working or a way to ask to go for a walk. One of those options may meet Joe's need better. Matt will be more satisfied when he can see a menu of choices and say more of the names.

Teach these words at the time the student needs them. . .in the middle of real situations. Teach the words by modeling them and use visual tools to help the students remember what to say.

It is often stated that students with autism do not generalize well. They have difficulty transferring a skill learned in one setting to use in a different situation. Generalization becomes less problematic when functional vocabulary is taught in the context of real, meaningful situations. Try to capture the moment. It is most ideal to watch the student and anticipate his need so you can teach the words before he begins to use negative behaviors.

PROBLEM: When people greet Todd, he doesn't answer them.

CAUSE: Todd doesn't know what to say.

SOLUTION: Give Todd some suggestions and give him a chance to practice using them.

Things to say to people

1. Hi

2. How are you?

3. What's happening?

4. What's up?

5. Give me five!

When someone comes in the room...

say HI

Say GOODBYE when someone leaves

PROBLEM: Ron knows how to talk, but in pressure situations he gets flustered and takes too long or forgets what he needs to say. He can't remember what to say and he ends up repeating a lot of delayed echolalia that does not accomplish his purpose.

CAUSE: It takes Ron a long time to process language. It is difficult for him to focus and retrieve the exact words he wants to or needs to use. That is the way his brain functions.

SOLUTION: If Ron can see something to help him remember, he can speak more quickly and remember what he needs to say. Cue cards help him use his language more successfully in those pressure situations.

ORDER A LARGE PIZZA

PEPPERONI

HAM

GREEN PEPPERS

Say: → I don't know

Say: → I don't want to play

Things to Say

Things to say when you want to talk to someone.

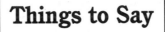

Hi	What's up?	How are you?

Give me 5	Guess what?	Hello
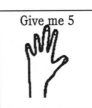		

PROBLEM: Gina looks attentive when people ask her questions, but she always quickly answers with "I don't know". She doesn't give correct answers even if she knows them.

CAUSE: Gina has developed a habit of taking her turn too quickly. She responds so fast that she doesn't allow herself enough time to try to find the answer.

SOLUTION: Instead of saying "I don't know" Gina needs to say something else to keep the conversation going while she thinks of an answer. Giving her a menu of choices will help her select a more appropriate response. Then she can participate with more variety in her conversation.

THE POINT IS: We need to teach words that will enable students to gain power over their environments.

Students will use language instead of behavior to get their needs met if the language works better than the behavior.

It is critical to teach the words and appropriate communication behaviors that will replace inappropriate behaviors.

Instead of saying "I don't know."
you can say :

1. I can't remember.
2. I haven't thought about that.
3. I'm not sure.
4. I need time to think.
5. I need help with that one.
6. I would rather not discuss that.
7. Yes.
8. No.
9. I don't know the answer.

COMMUNICATING FEELINGS

One of the most common desires for educators and parents is for students to *"learn to communicate their feelings."* The anticipation is that if students can share more about how they feel, they will be less likely to demonstrate inappropriate behaviors. If they could tell us how they feel, we would not have to do so much guessing. Unfortunately, teaching this skill is more complicated than it seems it should be. Even adults can have difficulty expressing their emotions and discomforts. That is why our society is full of counselors and support groups and even famous radio talk shows all designed to help people learn.

This is a complicated issue with vague answers. The goal here is to explore this area of communication in relation to the topics in this book: behavior, communication and visual strategies.

Why is communicating feelings so difficult?

Describing feelings is a very abstract activity. Mastering the ability to communicate these abstract concepts is difficult for many people, not just students with social and communication disabilities.

Isn't this exactly the area that students with autism spectrum disorders have difficulty with?

Yes! This is a main deficit area for these students. Some students are more capable than others in their ability to communicate feelings and emotions, however, by the definition of autism, this will be a challenging area for all of them. Successful socialization depends on developing some effective skills here.

What skills are important to teach?

The major reason people want to teach feelings is because they expect it will help modify behavior situations. When students get upset it would be nice to know why, so we can do something about it. When students are sick or tired it would be nice to know the reason for their discontent. People presume that if the student can tell you how he feels, that will make things better. They expect being able to label a mental state. . . "I am disappointed" or "I am bored". . . will fix the situation. It probably won't.

The best skills to teach are those that will help students better handle those emotional events in their lives. That means we need to begin by teaching skills for very specific problems and situations. Being able to *label* a state of mind is not as important as teaching communication skills that will:

- give him appropriate ways to express his state of mind

- help the student handle challenging or emotional situations to get his wants and needs met

> *When we think about emotions, it is easy to focus on bad feelings or negative situations. Remember that many emotional states are positive. Even positive emotional states can result in inappropriate behavior.*

I work with high skilled students. My students talk a lot and have a lot of academic skills. What about them?

Don't be fooled by academic achievement. Accomplishing a level of skill in reading or math does not guarantee successful emotional expression. In fact, a student who is more advanced academically can experience greater difficulty in this area because people expect that he should be more capable than he is. *It is critical to remember that a student's academic level may be totally different from his skill for communicating feelings in highly charged social/emotional situations.* Performing complicated functions on a computer does not guarantee the ability to express abstract emotional concepts.

Even though they may have more language for general conversation, higher skilled students may not be able to use that language to effectively communicate in social/emotional situations. Particularly in moments of great emotion or frustration or stress, they may not be able to draw upon the language they use at other times. The frustration of not being able to verbally handle situations frequently leads to greater frustration or behavior outbursts.

> *The expression of emotion is generally closely tied to trying to make a request or protest. The labeling of an emotion is a very abstract skill. Communicating the request or protest that links to an emotional state is considerably more concrete. Blending these skills together may produce the most success for our students.*

EXPRESSING COMMON EMOTIONS

Students tend to express a narrow range of emotions. Some of the classics are:

Happy which means I am content and life is good. It may have an appearance of great joy in laughter, or it may appear as intense interest in the activity of the moment.

Upset is usually represented with whining, crying or protest. It occurs when I don't get my way, when I am uncomfortable or when anything is not as I desire it to be.

Mad represents the extreme protest. Exaggerated crying or other body communication such as flailing arms and legs, commonly labeled temper tantrums, is the common expression of this. Physical aggression is another extreme protest.

Fear is experienced and expressed for the unfamiliar or when something negative is anticipated. It may be represented by crying or protest as a means of escape or as a way to generate comfort.

Pain or **sick** can be any physical discomfort ranging from a slight bump or a wet diaper to a major agony from toothaches to fevers or broken bones. Pain or sick may be communicated by a continuum of responses from seeking comfort, whining or crying, to major tantrums or physical aggression.

Tired is a condition that is frequently fought by students. It can totally change their ability to handle situations that would not be a problem if they were in a non-tired state. A common reaction to being tired is to become upset or mad, which can be represented in the ways listed above.

Hunger is a frequently reoccurring need. How this is communicated will vary significantly among children.

Think of youngsters as having a menu of choices to express themselves. Babies have a very limited number of choices on their menu because they have limited communication means. As children mature, they gradually add to their list of options by increasing their ability to communicate a greater variety of responses.

When something happens that demands an emotional response, the child goes to his *menu of choices* to choose a reaction. If you realize that most of the choices on this limited menu are represented by some form of crying or protest, it becomes more clear why students consistently respond to situations negatively. The obvious goal that emerges is to increase the number of choices on the student's menu.

CHOOSING VOCABULARY

What you are really suggesting is increasing the student's vocabulary. How do you figure out what words to teach?

Part of the disability in autism spectrum disorders, is difficulty reading and understanding social cues. Because this is a challenging area for these students, *stick to the basics*. Unless you are working with students who have a lot of language and a high level of understanding, it is better to target those nice generic vocabulary words: happy, sad, mad, afraid. Add to that list those words that describe the most common needs: hungry, tired, and sick. If those specific words do not meet your needs, choose similar words that convey general situations. Even though that is not a highly sophisticated list, those words will apply to a large percentage of circumstances that students encounter.

It is better to work consistently with a smaller number of words that students can learn to use competently than to introduce a larger variety that causes confusion. Remember, it takes a high level of social understanding to be able to discern the difference between feelings such as disgusted or embarrassed or confused.

COMMUNICATING EMOTIONS

What is the best way to teach students to communicate their feelings or needs to others?

Capture the moment. Teach the vocabulary they need to learn *while they are in the midst of real situations.*

- If a student is expressing emotion with his behavior, tell him with words and pictures what he is experiencing.

- Guide him to know what to communicate.

- Show him how to make a request or protest that will help the problem.

Labeling the emotional state is a small part of solving the problem. The most important part of handling emotional situations is taking some kind of action to attempt to change the situation. Making requests, communicating protest, or choosing something different are successful ways to modify those emotional situations.

SAMPLES & EXAMPLES

SITUATION: Trent kept pushing his work away and sliding off his chair to the floor. Every time the teacher asked him to get back into his chair he slapped the floor and yelled "NO". He kept yelling things like, "I don't have to do work!" "Work is stupid." Noticing dark circles under Trent's eyes, the teacher began to hypothesize that he was either not feeling well or was tired.

CAUSE: The teacher didn't know for sure. Sometimes it is not clear why a student is having difficulty. If we don't know, we have to hypothesize what the problem is. We need to begin to investigate like Sherlock Holmes. The teacher asked Trent some questions to get more information. "Do you feel sick?" "Are you tired?" The answers she got did not clearly indicate the problem. Then she pulled out some pictures and began to ask more specific questions, "Where does it hurt? Does your leg hurt? Does your stomach hurt?" "Do you want to sleep?" When she asked the question about sleep, Trent connected. He started saying some things about bed.

A common teaching technique is to have students label picture cards of peoples faces that are demonstrating different emotional states. The problem with this type of activity is that the student may learn to label the picture card but not understand how that emotion is expressed in real life. Learning to label the picture card does not ensure he knows what to do or how to respond when he encounters someone expressing the emotions. The labeling activity does not teach him how to handle his own emotional challenges.

SOLUTION: Once the teacher had a clear sense of Trent's need, she did three important things.

She *told* him how he was feeling. "Trent is tired." "Trent wants to sleep." Using the pictures, she encouraged Trent to tell her he was tired and wanted sleep.

Next, she gave him some options: you can put your head down on your desk or you can sit in the relaxing chair.

After the event, the teacher went back to talk with Trent again. She used her pictures again to talk with Trent about how he was tired. He chose the relaxing chair. Now he feels good and can do his work. She might even put it in a story form.

Even if Trent could not talk, the teacher would go through the same procedure of telling him how he was feeling, giving him choices, and reviewing the situation afterwards. The visual tools would still be the center of these conversations.

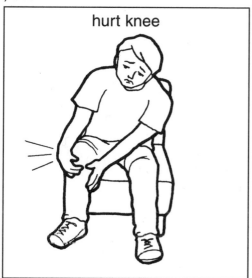

hurt knee

tired

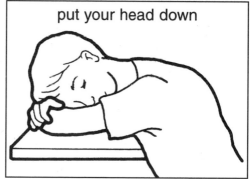

put your head down

sit in the relaxing chair

PROBLEM: Casey was whining. He began leaning over to bite people, banging his head and a few other behaviors that he had not engaged in for years. Casey couldn't talk, so he wasn't able to tell anyone what his problem was.

CAUSE: This is another situation where no one is quite sure why Casey is having a problem. Careful observation revealed that Casey was rubbing his ear a lot. The hypothesis was that Casey had an earache.

SOLUTION: The most important part of the solution was seeking medical treatment. The doctor confirmed an ear infection. Once that was confirmed, Mom used words and pictures to tell Casey what his problem was. Then she helped Casey use the picture to tell Dad that he had an earache. She encouraged Casey to communicate that message to every person in his life that day. Sometimes you don't know what the problem is, but when you do know for sure, make it a teaching moment.

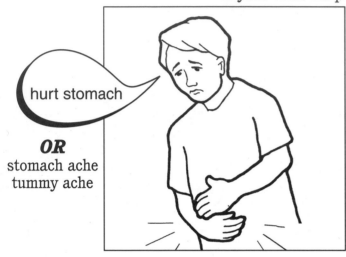

hurt stomach

OR
stomach ache
tummy ache

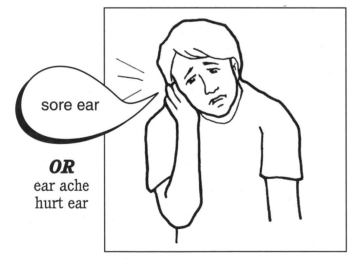

sore ear

OR
ear ache
hurt ear

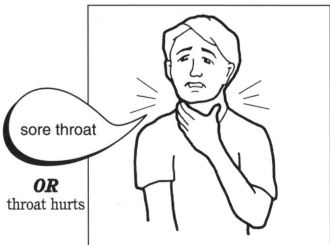

sore throat

OR
throat hurts

There are several different phrases that could be used to describe a child's discomfort. Pick the one you think will work best for the student and write it on the picture card. Try writing it with the words he could say.

PROBLEM: Darren's favorite older brother joined the military. After the brother left home, Darren wandered and cried and questioned about him daily.

CAUSE: Darren was missing his brother.

SOLUTION: This is a perfect time to teach more communication. Darren was sad because he missed his brother. Tell him how he feels with words and pictures. Students with a lot of verbal skills will express how they feel. Darren doesn't know how to do that. Talking about it can help ease the emotion. Write it down so you can talk about it again later.

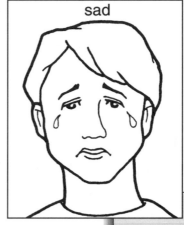

sad

Establish a hypothesis and teach the vocabulary

There are those times when you don't know what the problem or need is. Sometimes you can check out the situation. For example, the school nurse may verify if a student has a fever. A call home may reveal more information about his health or his state of fatigue. Even with research, there are times you just have to guess. . . .your best educated guess. Then give the student some options that can be paired with your guess. When your guess seems quite accurate, be sure to use that as an opportunity to teach more vocabulary.

> Bob is in the army.
>
> Bob went far away to Georgia.
>
> Bob won't come home for a long time.
>
> That makes Darren sad.

This is the kind of vocabulary that will be most meaningful to students when taught in the midst of real situations. Try to capture as many opportunities as you can to associate the real situations with a visual representation and the right vocabulary. Ideally you would talk with a student about how he feels when the situation is beginning. Sometimes that is possible, but if he is really upset, you may not get much language from him then. That is why it is so important to *retell the situation* after it is done.

happy

THE POINT IS:
- Regardless of the level of a student's language development, he may not be able to adequately express himself in stressful or highly emotional situations

- Visual strategies help students handle emotional communication more effectively

- Considering the challenge, there are many students who do learn skills to enable them to express a range of emotional information and have consideration for the feelings of others

> Bob is going to call on the telephone on Sunday.
>
> That makes Darren happy.

Chapter 11

Tools To Support Self-Management

When students are younger, it is necessary for adults to provide the structure and routine for their lives. Adults also provide the support to manage the behavior difficulties that students encounter. The long-range goal is for students to gain the ability to manage themselves independently. That means learning how to manage their own behavior in an acceptable fashion. It also means managing their time and personal life routines appropriately. Visual tools provide excellent support to accomplish these goals.

TEACHING SKILLS FOR SELF REGULATION

My students rely on me to tell them what to do when there is a problem. Will they always need that external guidance?

Our students easily become dependent on us to tell them what to do. We teach them to follow our directions, but we may not teach them to make choices and decisions to help themselves. They will benefit if we teach them to monitor their own behavior and needs. A valuable goal is to teach students to make decisions for themselves. Many students can learn some skills that will help.

How do you teach them to monitor themselves? Isn't that hard to do?

This is a difficult skill for many people, not just students with special needs. When people are bothered or upset, it is natural to react to whatever is causing the problem. In the middle of that emotional reaction it is necessary to stop and make a decision to change something to respond to the situation differently. This can be extremely confusing for our students with behavior and communication difficulties. In the best of circumstances they may experience problems making decisions and communicating their needs. When they are required to do it in a state of stress, it can become almost impossible.

What do you recommend teaching?

It is impossible to teach a technique for every possible problem the student may encounter. In general, students benefit from the following:

- Helping them recognize that they are having a difficulty or need

- Giving them an opportunity to independently make different choices

- Teaching students to determine when they are calm or ready to do something different

What do you do? How do you teach students to handle their problems themselves?

Remember that these students benefit from learning routines. They benefit from visual cues and prompts. Therefore, a logical solution would be to use visual supports to give students prompts and to teach them some routines. This approach will not solve every situation, but it will be a beginning toward helping students handle themselves more independently. Remember, the more they can handle without someone telling them what to do, the more successful they will be. Here are some examples.

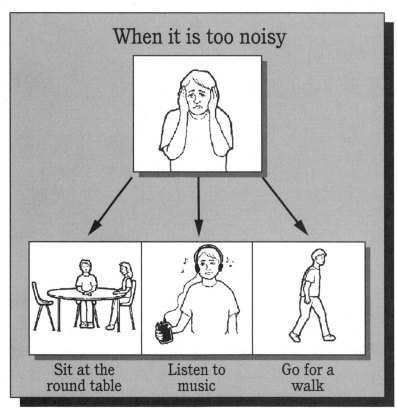

When it is too noisy

Sit at the round table   Listen to music   Go for a walk

SAMPLES & EXAMPLES

PROBLEM: Carlos was very sensitive to loud sounds. At times the classroom became too noisy for him to control himself comfortably. When the room noise increased, Carlos was apt to begin crying, biting his wrist, or hitting other students. He didn't know what else to do to handle the situation.

CAUSE: Carlos was reacting to the sound in the only way he knew. He didn't know how to change the environment.

SOLUTION: Carlos needed to learn how to manage himself differently during those uncomfortable times. The teacher worked with him to help him learn some language to communicate the problem. A communication tool was developed to prompt appropriate language for the situation. In addition, the teacher gave him several alternatives he could choose when he was losing control. In the beginning she needed to show Carlos what the options were and help him select one. Once Carlos learned it was OK to choose a different option, he began to choose those options when something was bothering him.

When it is too noisy...

Say  Can I take a break?

 Then decide what to do

Quiet 1. Go to the quiet area

Earphones 2. Wear earphones

Music 3. Listen to music

Walk   4. Go for a walk

PROBLEM: Bob has difficulty handling unstructured time. He wanders and flaps his arms and starts to pace back and forth. Then he tries to play with the dog, but he does things that make the dog growl.

CAUSE: Bob requires a lot of structure. He doesn't seem to remember what his options are. He has difficulty choosing an appropriate activity to do with the dog.

SOLUTION: Teach Bob to make a choice. Give him some reminders so he can make an appropriate choice about what to do with the dog. Bob would benefit from choice menus for various times during his day. Teach him to select something from the choice menu when he has nothing to do. The long-term goal would be for Bob to go make a selection from the menu independently.

PROBLEM: Many students become upset for countless reasons. Once they become upset, it can be difficult for them to calm down without an adult monitoring their behavior.

SOLUTION: Use a visual tool to guide the student into a calming routine. Use the tool as the reminder of appropriate behavior. Once the student learns what the visual tool represents, just the presence of that tool may be enough to remind the student of what behavior to exhibit. Consider these examples.

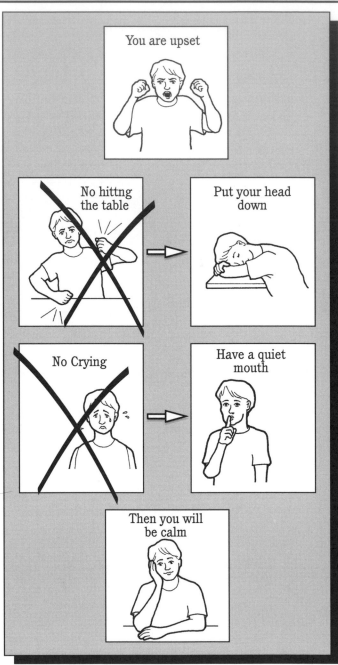

If something is bothering you

Relax

1.  Move away

2. Take 5 deep breaths

3.  Come back to the table

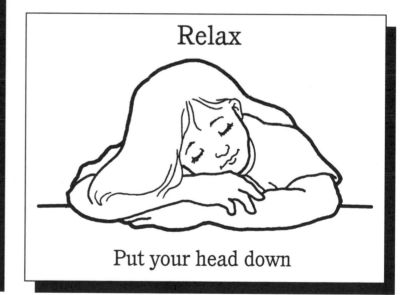

Relax

Put your head down

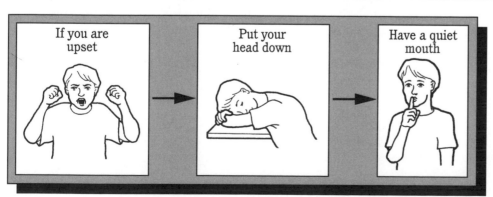

If you are upset → Put your head down → Have a quiet mouth

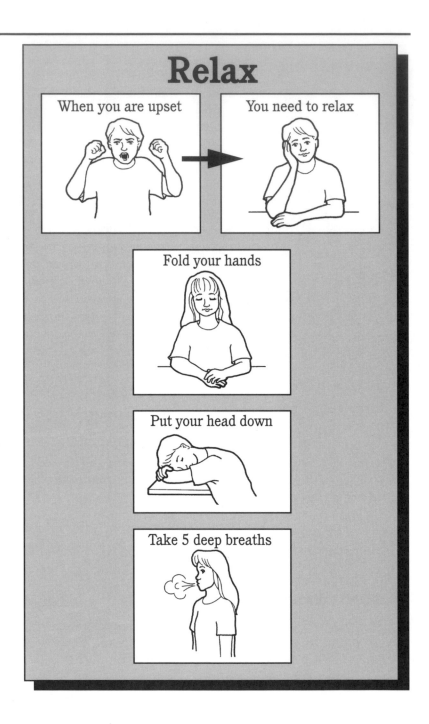

When you are upset

You need to relax

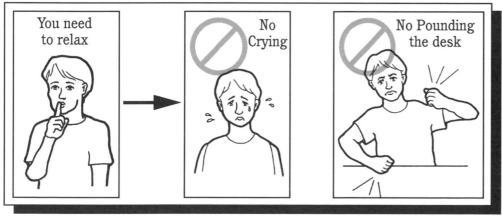

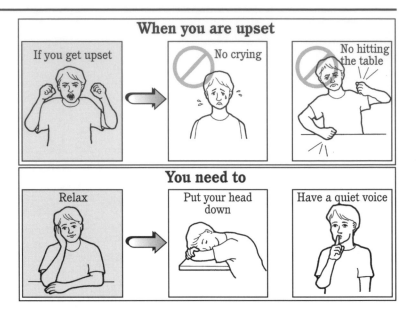

The long term goal is to teach students some strategies that will help them handle themselves appropriately in difficult situations. Giving them some rules and direction guides then to make appropriate behavior choices during stressful or upsetting incidents.

THE POINT IS: Students benefit from:

- being able to monitor and change their own behavior
- learning routines and making choices to help them handle difficult situations
- using visual tools to help support the learning of independent skills

Part 5

IMPLEMENTING VISUAL TOOLS AND SUPPORT

The book *Visual Strategies for Improving Communication* contains extensive information about how to develop visual tools. See appendix for more information.

This visual approach makes sense for my students. I guess I need to find some pictures!

Remember that your own body and real objects are your most easily accessed visual supports. Your second resource is things already in your environment. Look around you. There are visual supports everywhere!

After using those resources, it may be appropriate to develop some other visual tools to help manage behavior situations or give students information. More and more people are coming to understand the value of using visual supports. Once they acknowledge the value of this approach, they are faced with figuring out how to do it.

Chapter 12

Developing Visual Tools

What kind of visuals should I use? How do you decide between using real objects, photos, line drawings, written language, or other variations?

This is a common question. Occasionally, heated differences of opinion begin to erupt as teachers and programs attempt to develop systems and "standardize" what they use. There are no fixed rules. What is appropriate will vary from one student to the next. There may be diverse needs in a classroom. Consider these thoughts:

1. Use what the student can understand *quickly and easily*. This is the most critical criteria for deciding what visual forms to use. Any time a student has to take the time to try to figure out what something means, the flow of communication is interrupted. If you have to spend too much time teaching a student what a visual tool means, it is probably too difficult and needs to be in a simpler form. *When in doubt, use something simpler or more concrete.* Remember that the goal is to improve understanding.

2. Consider the age and functioning level of the student. Younger students and lower skilled students generally need more photographs or real concrete objects. Your first goal is to have students participate. If things are too difficult for them, they won't learn as quickly. As students develop more skill, they will learn to understand a greater variety of visual forms. *The most common mistake is starting too high... with picture forms that students don't understand easily.*

3. Remember that *real* is more concrete than other options. Drawings can range from realistic to very abstract. The more abstract drawings are, the more difficult it is for students to learn to recognize them or understand them. The real picture from the package of a child's favorite cookie will elicit more enthusiasm than a drawing of a generic cookie.

4. Don't be afraid of mixed forms. Everything does not have to be the same. All pictures do not have to be the same size or from the same clip art program. In fact, a mixture can actually make them easier to recognize. A student's communication system can include any variety of visual supports, as long as he understands what they mean.

- Why not use the real logos and labels from stores, food items, TV shows, videos, fast food restaurants and other easily available and easily recognizable community advertising?

- Take photos with a camera or digital camera of the real objects and people in a student's life.

- Save the more abstract drawings for those things that are more abstract and can't be represented easily in a realistic picture or photo.

- Use written language for speed and ease if a student understands it.

- Pictures paired with written words are generally an ideal choice.

One of the biggest controversies is whether or not to use pictures for students who can read. Certainly using written language is easier than finding pictures. Written language is a great emergency tool. But most students benefit from pictures integrated into visual supports. Yes, they can read, but our goal in using visual tools is to achieve quick, immediate recognition. Most students can do that better with picture-word combinations than with words alone. Just think about how the advertising world communicates with us. They know we will instantly recognize their images and logos. That is the type of recognition we want our students to experience.

5. Use what works. Watch how students respond. If they don't understand quickly and easily, reevaluate what visual form you are using. You may need something different. As students get older they can understand more varieties and variations. That does not mean that you have to make things more difficult for them. It just means you have more options. *There is no reward for making things too difficult for students.*

6. Teach something that works and then move on. There are some teachers who feel obligated to teach progressively more abstract or more difficult versions of the same thing. Rather than re-teaching the same skill over and over with more abstract visual representations, use the time to teach the student a greater variety of new communication skills.

7. Use what works for a whole group. When planning visual tools for a class of students, consider using representations that everyone will understand. If some understand drawings and others require photos, use photos for those visual tools that will support the whole class. That way everyone can understand them. Photos will not hurt the more capable students. Then, when you are developing visual supports for individual students, you can integrate more abstract art for those students who understand it.

8. Use what is easy. If time is short, use what you have. Be creative. ***Any* visual support is generally better than *no* visual support.**

9. Make visual tools simple but complete. If visual tools need to be explained, they are too complex. Write the script or words you say when using the tool. Tools should be self explanatory; easy for anyone to understand. If the adults don't understand them, the students won't.

10. Become spontaneous. Become a communication partner who supports your communication visually. Use gestures. Point to things. Hold up objects. Whenever you are telling something to a student, try to support your communication visually with a variety of forms. Use whatever is within reach.

11. Remember your goals. Your goal is to become a better communication partner. Another goal is to create a communication rich environment. Communication interactions will improve with visual supports as long as the student understands what those supports are communicating.

> *The biggest mistake people make is to use visual forms that are too difficult for students to understand easily. When in doubt, make it simple.*

> *Remember, the purpose of using visual supports is to improve understanding and reduce behavior problems. Developing visual tools that are too difficult for a student to comprehend will not help the problem and may actually make things worse.*

HOW TO USE VISUAL SUPPORTS TO ENHANCE COMMUNICATION

Think of a three-step approach:

1. Show to get their attention

2. Tell in simple language

3. Make sure they understand

Don't forget to *teach* students what the visual tools mean. Even though students have a comparative strength in understanding visual information, do not presume they will understand anything you put in front of them. Teaching means showing or demonstrating exactly what the tools are communicating. Make sure they understand what the visual tools mean.

What is the most important thing to remember about using visual supports?

Remember to use them. Try to develop a style of communicating that is visually supported. Become a visual communicator. Try this experiment: Teach your class for a while without talking. Pretend you have laryngitis for the day. What do you need to do to communicate with the students? You will probably become a visual communicator very naturally. How do the students respond? They probably understand quite well. This experiment demonstrates how you want to communicate even when you are using speech.

Why do visual tools fail?

There are occasions when visual tools do not accomplish what we intend. The main reasons visual tools fail are:

- They are not in *forms* that students understand

- They don't contain the right information

- People make them but don't use them

> *Remember that students with autism are known for their visual strength. That means they may be able to recognize abstract drawings because they recognize them as geometric designs. Labeling a design is very different from understanding the meaning that a picture represents. Even though they learn to identify or label those drawings, they may not really understand the meaning.*

> *Make the preparation of visual tools a teaching time. Students frequently benefit from participating in the creation of visual tools. Have them help you decide what pictures to use or what the tools should say. The more input the student has, the more invested he will be. This approach will not work for all students, but it is a highly successful technique for those who will understand.*

Chapter 13

Addressing Special Needs

Evaluating behavior situations and planning communication support for students requires understanding the student's unique needs. The student's age, overall skill levels, and level of communication development are critical factors when assessing situations. The techniques and strategies in this book can be adapted to apply to many of the behavior situations that occur.

Do visual strategies always work? You have presented valuable tools to modify behavior problems for a lot of students. Do these strategies work for all students? Are there situations where they will not work?

The use of visual strategies is a valuable option for changing the behavior and supporting the communication of *most* students. Even though we have determined that a large percentage of students with communication disabilities are visual learners, all of them are not. But, even many students whose major strength is not visual can still benefit from the use of visual supports as *a part of* their communication system. It is always critical to assess which areas an individual student functions most effectively in. Identifying his strengths allows you to develop programming to utilize those strengths.

A common teaching approach suggests you *teach to the student's strengths and remediate his weaknesses.* There is logic in this way of thinking. Using teaching and communication strategies that allow a student to use his primary skill areas will give him the greatest opportunity to participate and succeed. Many behavior difficulties arise because students are not given the opportunity to use and develop their strongest abilities.

Remediating weaknesses is a noble goal. Students can learn to function better in their weaker areas, however, care should be taken to keep this goal in perspective. Consider these thoughts:

- Activities to remediate weaknesses are not a prerequisite to teaching to the student's strengths. Any teaching designed to strengthen weak skills should be a supplement to the primary goal of using the student's strengths to teach those most important communication skills that he needs to modify behavior challenges.

- *Remember that students with behavior challenges require **immediate** solutions to their difficulties.* Make sure to prioritize your teaching objectives so you are spending your time teaching those skills that will be most necessary to change the student's behavior. Many remediation activities are designed to teach global skills that will hopefully improve over a long period of time. That is not enough when you are dealing with immediate behavior difficulties.

- Recognize that the student's weaknesses may always be there. By definition they are a part of his disability. They may never be *fixed* or *cured*. Certainly we want a student to maximize his abilities in all areas; however, establishing priorities is critical, especially when we are dealing with significant problems.

- Don't forget long term planning. Working on some of those weaker skills may actually be more successful when the student gets older. If earlier training focuses on teaching to his strengths, the student will develop a level of communication skill and appropriate behavior that will support learning other skills more efficiently when he is a bit older.

Are there any students who require special consideration?

Yes, there are some special groups of students that may require adjustments in planning and approach.

Very Young Children

Dealing with the behavior problems of young children is challenging because they simply do not understand very well. When viewing all the varieties of visual tools, it is critical to recognize that many of them are too complicated for very young children. For the youngest population, the best visual strategies are real objects and your gestures and body language. After you make a communication connection you can gradually add more options. Just be warned that the greatest error that people make is to get too complicated too quickly. They present things to young children that are too advanced for the students to understand.

Students with Limited Cognitive Ability

The students who function in the lower range of ability will learn more slowly than other students will. The behaviors they demonstrate may match their mental age more than their chronological age. Considering that, it is important to make sure to use visual strategies that match what the student will understand. Very often gestures, body language and real objects are the most successful. Even if students are older, they will probably understand the simpler, more concrete visual strategies better. Recognizing their slower learning rate, it is important to introduce new visual tools very gradually and thoroughly teach what they mean.

Programming for Older Students and Adults

Visual strategies are tools for life. *There is no need to try to fade them out or extinguish their use.* In fact, visual tools provide the support necessary for greater independence in adulthood.

It is possible to begin using visual tools with older students, even if they have not used these strategies before. If older students have not been introduced to visual tools before, it is important to remember *that they will need to be taught what the tools mean.* When introducing visual tools to modify behaviors, remember how long the student has been exhibiting the behaviors you are attempting to change. The longer they have used the inappropriate behaviors, the longer it will take to make changes. Older students will benefit from the same teaching strategies that work for younger students.

Students with Visual Impairment

Discussions about using visual strategies for students with autism acknowledge that there are some students diagnosed with autism who are also visually impaired or blind. Providing visual strategies for a student who cannot see does seem questionable. It is always desirable to identify which senses are most useful so you can teach to the student's strengths. When working with those students, consider the following:

1. Find out how much vision is functional for the student. A student who is legally blind may still have some vision. What can he see? Color or shape or some details? Can he see better when using a light box? (When pictures are placed on a lighted box, some students can see items better).

2. Explore how students are able to interpret larger pictures or visual tools compared to smaller ones.

3. Realize that objects may be a better option than pictures.

4. Consider the basic principles discussed in this book as guides for assessing the student's behavior and communication. Remember that the communication approach in this book encourages using a variety of visual forms to support communication.

Students with Multiple Disabilities or Unknown Diagnoses

Regardless of the diagnosis or educational label a student has been given, it is still important to identify the *causes* of his behavior differences. The approach to dealing with behavior problems will still follow the procedure of targeting the behavior, identifying the cause, and looking for the communication components as a part of the solution. Educational and diagnostic labels are pieces of information that help us understand the student better. Identifying his specific communication difficulties and needs in relationship to his behavior problems will be a key to making positive changes.

Students with Extreme Behaviors

There are some students who demonstrate extreme behaviors; either excessive in frequency or extreme in violence, self-abuse or some quality that prevents the student from participating adequately in life routines. These are situations that require a strong team approach. All the possible causes of behavior problems need to be considered individually and in combination. The solutions for lasting change generally require a combination of efforts because there are typically multiple causes. One of the intervention strategies that is easily forgotten when dealing with these extreme cases is accommodating for the student's ability to understand. Most management programs for these students are handled with lots of verbal language. Providing strong visual communication support is a very critical consideration when dealing with these students. Visual tools provide support for both the students and the adults who are implementing the management strategies.

THE POINT IS: Visual strategies support the communication needs of students to successfully improve communication and modify behavior problems. The positive effects of this approach will be achieved by remembering:

- how we prepare visual tools affects how successfully they will accomplish their purpose.

- integrating the use of visual supports into our own communication interactions is critically important.

- the visual approach needs to be adapted to meet individual student needs and learning styles.

Part 6

THE QUESTIONS AND CONCERNS

C h a p t e r

14

What To Do When Things Don't Go Well

In spite of all our planning and strategizing, there are times when the students still have difficulties. Remember that they are human. It is normal for people to have better days and worse days. It is normal to experience challenges, not feel well or just plain be obstinate.

AARRGGH!

Do you ever have days when you feel like a complete failure? You are doing everything you know to do and it isn't working?

Let's be honest. No matter how much we plan. . . no matter how much we structure, we all have experienced those days that we don't wish to remember.

How do you avoid having tantrums or other serious problems?

Our first goal is to provide our students with the support necessary to *avoid* difficulties. As students improve their understanding and have predictable routines, they will be more able to participate effectively at home and at school. When necessary medical interventions and sensory accommodations are designed to meet the student's needs, there can be significant differences in their ability to handle their life routines. We need to make sure the basics are in place. But, in spite of all these efforts, there will still be situations or days when life just doesn't go as planned.

What do you do to handle a tantrum or other "blow-up"?

Tantrums, aggression and other escalating behaviors, can occur for numerous reasons including:

- as forms of communication

- students trying to get what they want

- protesting something

- as a response to a communication breakdown

- when students lose control

- when students reach a point of extreme frustration or exhaustion

- because that is a pattern or learned behavior for a specific circumstance

When an extreme problem does occur or when a crisis erupts, the first goal is for the student to calm down. It will be difficult for any effective communication to take place until there is some calm. Since each student can be so different, there is no magic formula, however, consider these ideas.

> *When a student is having a huge problem, it can be critically important to figure out why. Understanding why will be the key to your ultimate solution. Sometimes it is necessary to quickly survey the situation and form a temporary hypothesis until you have the opportunity to get all the information. In the meantime, the calming techniques are designed to manage the situation so no one gets hurt. Once the student has gained some stability, you will then have the opportunity to more thoroughly assess the situation and choose a remedy.*

> *Keep in mind that there will be times when you may never be able to determine why.*

Neutral behaviors are designed to get the student to do something positive that will begin to diffuse the current difficulty. They could include:

- *fold your hands*
- *stand up*
- *sit*
- *go sit in a quiet area*
- *leave the room*
- *put your head down*
- *have a quiet mouth*
- *pick something up*
- *hold an object*
- *release an object*
- *put something down*

CALMING TECHNIQUES

1. Communicate clearly what the student needs to do

Visually communicate what the student needs to do to calm or stop the inappropriate behavior. Use pictures, gestures or other visual supports to show the student what to do.

- **Try to engage the student in a "neutral" behavior.** Neutral behaviors are designed to stop the negative behavior and help the student regain control. If he is engaging in the neutral behavior, the student can't be doing the inappropriate behavior, or at least it will be somewhat modified.

- OR, **Make it clear what the student is supposed to be doing.** Communicate a request or direction to get the student engaged in the activity that was occurring when the behavior erupted. Be sure to support your directions visually.

2. Talk less

Use very little language. Give a simple verbal direction paired with visual supports and then be quiet. When students are having difficulties, there is a huge temptation to talk more; explaining or giving directions. If the student is out of control, the extra verbal bombardment can serve to escalate his behavior even more. Students who are sensitive to sound can become super-hyper-sensitive in times of frustration. Generally, limited language works best, however, there are a few students who recoup better and faster if verbal language is totally eliminated and only visual forms of communication are used.

3. Use yourself as a visual tool

Your body language, stance, position, and facial expressions will visually demonstrate to the student what you expect him to do.

- **Use your body to make things happen**
  Look like you are expecting the student to respond. Look like you are ready. Hold out your hand. Point to what the student is supposed to do. Hold out the object of contention. Wait expectantly.

- **Use your body to communicate what should not happen**
  Push away an item of dispute, fold your arms and shake your head, or use other gestures to make your point.

- **Use your body to prevent things from happening**
  Position yourself to prevent a problem. Standing between the student and an object, blocking a doorway or sitting in a location that keeps the student in a specific area are ways to control difficulties. Avoid turning your back to the student.

> *It is particularly important to keep your attention on a student and not turn your back on him when there is a significant problem. That can be an open invitation for physical aggression.*

4. Wait

Once you have communicated what the student needs to do, wait. When everything is going well, these students frequently need some "wait" time during communication interactions. At times of distress, that need for wait time may increase. Wait expectantly. Continue to *show* the student what he needs to do. The visual supports will keep communicating even if you are not talking.

5. Be aware of eye contact

Students can be remarkably aware of your attention or the attention of others to their behavior. Sometimes, looking at them serves to give attention that will perpetuate their actions. If attention seems to be contributing to the problem, change something. Try looking away, avoiding eye contact, changing your body orientation or moving some distance away from the student. This does not mean to totally leave a student or stop watching him. You must maintain visual awareness and an appropriate distance for safety. Be aware that adjusting your presence may help the situation.

6. Reduce the audience

Be aware that students who generally seem oblivious to their classmates or the people around them can become remarkably aware of their presence and attention during times of distress. There are some students that will take advantage of being out in the community. They may threaten to behave badly as a means of getting their own way in those environments. Do what you can to remove an audience that will reinforce bad behavior.

7. Avoid physical injury

Do not let students, their caregivers or others get injured. When students are having problems, it is very tempting to try to physically manage them. Use great caution when considering this option. Changing the situation by physically prompting a student can sometimes appear to be an easy solution. People commonly get close to students or physically help them in interventions such as:

- moving the student
- helping the student perform an action
- removing him from a situation
- removing him from a location
- removing an object that is instrumental in the problem
- attempting to stop physical aggression

> *There may be an occasion where there is an unexpected great risk of harm that requires immediate action. Although preplanning is ideal, in those situations, someone may be called on to act quickly using the best judgment and knowledge they have at that time. Fortunately, these situations are not common.*

Sometimes you have to move a student to prevent injury. At times, physical prompting or guidance is appropriate. In other situations, it may be unnecessary. It may even escalate a confrontation. Observe carefully what is happening. Be aware of the student's personal space. It is not unusual for a student's need for personal space to increase in the midst of a severe difficulty. Instead of jumping in with some form of physical maneuvering, a more effective response may be to stand back and give the student some space to collect himself. Then he will be ready do what is required.

There are some caregivers who are constantly getting hurt. This can be more common for new staff. They model "battle scars" from biting, scratching, pinching, head butting, and other student aggression. This should not happen. If a person is experiencing more than an occasional or accidental injury something needs to change quickly. It is time for a meeting and a new plan.

There may be times when physically prompting or moving a student is a part of the student's intervention plan. Just be aware of this:

- In times of distress, students who are sensitive to touch will probably be even more sensitive. Students may physically protest to avoid touch or being contained.

- It is not unusual for a student's need for personal space to increase when he is having a problem. Getting close when trying to physically prompt him may actually escalate his behavior.

- Because very young children do not understand well, physically managing them during behavior crisis situations is a natural reaction. Holding them, picking them up, or moving them to other locations are instinctive reactions. Techniques that work well for preschoolers will not be appropriate as students get older. Make sure your behavior intervention programs are working toward using techniques that will be appropriate as the student matures. Visual tools are frequently effective options.

8. Remind the student what he needs to do. . .then wait

Observe the student. It may be necessary to communicate your requests again. Perhaps several times. *Visually* remind the student what needs to be done. A reminder does not have to be verbal. Simply moving a visual tool or object or pointing again can be enough. Just avoid the temptation to bombard the student with repeated verbal requests.

9. As the student calms, prompt the appropriate behavior

Negotiate an acceptable ending to the event. This is a time to teach the student some appropriate alternatives to the inappropriate behavior.

- Help the student communicate the appropriate information for the situation.

- Show him a gesture or visual tool or teach the words that he needs to learn.

- Give him a choice.

- Redirect him to another activity.

- Guide him to complete the original activity.

10. Review, Reevaluate, Reinforce and Regroup

- Review the incident. . . .What happened? Why?

- Reevaluate how you handled it

- Reinforce yourself with help or different techniques for next time

- Regroup, take a deep breath (or 10 deep breaths) and go on

How long should you wait? How long does a tantrum last?

Each student will be different. When a student is fairly new to you, or you have not dealt with his upsets, it may seem that his demonstration of protest will keep going on forever. You can feel like the student will keep escalating and will never stop. In reality, it is not unusual for these behaviors to have a fairly predictable pattern. The student actually goes through a *routine* of escalation and de-escalation. This makes sense considering we are talking about students who learn routines and have difficulty changing routines.

In some cases, once a student begins the tantrum routine, he may need to follow the whole routine through until it is completed. Observe carefully so you will know what you might expect if a problem erupts again.

Does that mean you should just let an explosion run its course?

It may. It depends on the student. Of course, your first goal is prevention. But once a problem erupts, one of your goals is to observe. Pay attention to what you do that may actually escalate the student's behavior. Discover what cues or strategies you can use to calm the student or reduce the length of the event. The goal of calming techniques is to reduce the amount of time a student is in distress.

Do you have any cautions?

Be careful about what you do to try to get the tantrum to end. You may actually be creating an expected part of the routine. Then it won't end until you perform your part.

Example: Sammy has a tantrum every time Mom takes him to the grocery store. In embarrassment, she gives him a popsicle to help him calm down. Sammy begins to expect the popsicle every time he goes to the store. If Mom doesn't give him one, he may have a tantrum until he gets one. The popsicle becomes a symbol of the end of the tantrum.

OOPS! It is easy to fall into those patterns. Can you do things to shorten the tantrum?

One suggestion is to use a visual prop to indicate an end to the tantrum routine. Then you can visually show the student the prop and gradually introduce it earlier in the tantrum routine.

Example: If a student does some crying while having a tantrum, give him a tissue at the end to wipe his face. Next time he has a tantrum, get the tissue out and hold it in his view. Try to introduce it earlier in the tantrum routine. You may be able to develop a routine where the student will stop when he sees the tissue.

TISSUE

Using these incidents as teaching opportunities is essential. Students learn skills most quickly when we *capture the moment* and teach at the moment of real need.

Is there hope to make changes? Is there hope for better behavior?

Definitely yes!

1. The first goal would be to intervene to teach acceptable alternatives before the problem erupts. Discovering the causes of problems guides us toward prevention.

2. Once the student exhibits a major problem, work toward calming. Trying to teach a skill in the midst of an outburst will probably not be effective.

3. As the student calms, take advantage of the opportunity to teach a skill. These incidents are teaching opportunities for parents and educators, too. Continually evaluate how the student responds to what you are doing so you can decide what works best.

Remember: *If students get exactly what they want after a huge tantrum, they will remember the reward and be likely to utilize that communication form again.* Try using these opportunities to teach them more appropriate skills.

These steps are presented to give ideas to help diffuse those occasional intense or difficult moments. When a student develops a pattern of severe behavior, it is critical to thoroughly analyze the causes of that behavior so a plan can be designed to teach appropriate skills and provide the interventions or structure necessary to reduce opportunities for difficulties.

Author's note: Physically prompting and guiding students is a commonly used teaching technique. Physical management for behavior problems is different. There are strong opinions and regulations about physical management. Of course, families have different options than educators. For serious, persistent problems, a staffing to develop a behavior plan provides a critical framework to deal with the student's needs.

Chapter 15

Common Causes For Unsuccessful Behavior Management

Even though parents and educators have sincere intentions, there can be many times when their attempts to manage behavior situations are unsuccessful. It can feel like the problems are beyond our control. Here are a few reasons why our efforts may flounder.

1. Not looking at the "big picture"

Many behavior intervention approaches focus on extinguishing the viewed behavior without thoroughly evaluating its cause. *Identifying the cause is critically important for long term solutions.* Causes that are not immediately observable can relate significantly to the student's immediate behavior. The most effective solutions consider all the variables.

2. Failure to determine the true cause of the problem

In autism, there are three factors that are commonly interwoven into a large percentage of student behavior difficulties. The inability to *understand* effectively, *expressive communication* problems, and *sensory issues* are all common underlying causes of behavior difficulties. Communication impairments are also significant for many students with other diagnoses. To be most successful, a thorough assessment of behavior problems needs to consider these three areas as they relate to the situation.

3. Trying to deal with too many things at once

When students have lots of problems in lots of areas it can be overwhelming. When adults try to correct too many things simultaneously, both adults and students become frustrated. That is why identifying the cause of problems is so important. Frequently, focusing on changing the cause will result in changing multiple problems.

4. Spending your time taking data without actually finding functional solutions to problems

Data taking is the "official, formal, concrete" way to evaluate the fine details of the student's program. Data can give us helpful information about such things as how frequently a problem occurs or how long a tantrum lasts. When we are using new strategies or programs, data helps us determine if the student's behavior is changing. Beware, however, of creating situations where taking data gets in the way of teaching. *Data taking is not the program;* it is just a means to determine specifics of a situation. It helps us keep track of student performance. It helps us evaluate the success of an intervention. Observation is another way to gain valuable information.

5. Focusing on extinguishing behaviors rather than teaching skills

Telling students what *not to do* is sometimes helpful. Students need to be taught what *to do*. Students frequently use inappropriate behavior because they don't know what else to do. One of the most effective ways of reducing or eliminating inappropriate behavior is to teach the student a more effective and appropriate way to get his need met.

6. Presuming students understand

Many people recognize that behavior problems can occur because a student cannot express himself well. Fewer recognize that a student's difficulty *understanding* is frequently a significant source of behavior problems.

7. Failing to teach *functional* communication skills

For most behavior difficulties, communication emerges as a part of the problem or it becomes an essential part of the solution. If the behavior problem is related to the student's communication needs, then teaching more effective communication skills needs to be a major part of the solution. People frequently attempt to teach speech & language skills that are irrelevant or useless for altering the student's behavior.

8. Bombarding a student with too much verbal input, sensory input, or emotion

When students are having difficulty, it is tempting for the adults to do more. . .talk more, get closer to the student, or any reaction that intensifies the situation. Visual strategies can actually have a calming effect by helping maintain the student's attention without over-stimulating him.

9. Making the whole process too complicated

Although well intentioned, many behavior programs are not "user friendly" for parents or school staff. They may look impressive on paper. They utilize lots of fancy terminology and employ complex data sheets and paraphernalia; however, the people on the front line don't really understand what to do.

10. Reacting to difficult behaviors inconsistently

Students get confused easily. How do you figure out life if sometimes things work and sometimes they don't. Sometimes I get what I want and sometimes I get in trouble. It's frustrating, isn't it? The more inconsistent the adults are in managing behavior situations, the longer it will take to observe positive changes in the student's behavior.

11. Not getting the right amount of help

Dealing with behavior problems can be a complicated task. It can be exhausting. Evaluating yourself as a part of the situation is difficult. Different people will evaluate situations from different viewpoints. Teaming together with others helps keep the whole situation in perspective.

12. Not defining success

A teacher once asked, "Are we trying to make them "perfect" or are we trying to make them "normal"? She was referring to the behavior of her students with autism. She could see there is a wide range of what we call acceptable behavior from the regular student population and people were holding her students to a different standard. Success is not perfection. Think of success as appropriate participation.

13. Forgetting that kids are kids.

Just by their human nature students are going to have their ups and downs. Everything a student does is not a major problem. It takes discernment to sort out the things students do just because they are kids from the behaviors that are real problems.

14. Forgetting to have fun

Dealing with behavior problems is serious business. It is easy to focus on the behavior problems instead of the good times. Don't forget to enjoy the students when things are going well.

Chapter

16

Frequently Asked Questions

I want my child to talk. Won't using pictures keep my child from talking?

This is a common concern of parents whose children do not talk. Remember that a primary purpose for using pictures and other visual strategies to help students *understand* better. That is the goal for both verbal and non-verbal students. Visual strategies help reduce behavior problems. Then, when students are less frustrated, they become more ready to learn speech or other forms of communication.

When are students too old to start using visual supports?

It is never too late to begin supporting communication visually. The most important thing to remember is that older students and adults have not had the benefit of years of training to understand and use visual supports. Consequently, it may be necessary to start at the beginning; *don't presume they understand.* Also, remember that you may be attempting to change behavior patterns that have existed for many years. It will take time for the student to make changes. Rather than trying to change behavior patterns that have existed for many years, it is often easier to totally change things so you are teaching a whole new routine. Visual supports can help that happen.

Do you recommend using visual tools for everything a student does?

There are infinite ways that visual tools can be used to help students. What is critical, however, is providing the right amount of assistance. First, think of using visual supports to give general structure to a student's life. If there are parts of the student's life routines that work well, leave them alone and focus on providing visual support in areas where he experiences difficulty. Try to target areas of life where confusions or difficulties occur.

Won't using visual supports handicap my child?

He will be *more* handicapped by demonstrating behavior problems that prevent him from participating comfortably in his home and school environments. Remember that we all use and benefit from visually supported communication.

I am using a different behavior management program with my child. How does using visual supports fit in? Can I do both?

We use visual strategies for the purpose of improving communication. No matter what behavior program you are using, communication should be a critical consideration. The technique of using visual strategies to improve communication will support any well planned behavior program. Remember that many behavior problems have their roots in communication breakdowns. At times, visual tools can provide enough communication support for students so other behavior programs become unnecessary.

Will using visual strategies cure my child?

Visual tools do not cure a child's disability. They do provide the support that many students need to help them function more effectively in life. Visual strategies are not a magic Band-Aid. Even though using these techniques can produce highly effective results, they will not make up for bad programming, an inadequate curriculum, or inappropriate behavior management procedures.

How long will my student need to use visual supports?

When do I remove the visual tools?

How do I wean my child off visual the use of visual tools?

Do you use a calendar or daily planner to organize your schedule? Do you use them with the intent of eliminating from your life? Certainly not! They provide support for memory and organization of your daily activities.

Ponder the many functions that visual tools provide for students. Some students require lots of ongoing support. Other students may not need the visual supports on a regular basis, but may benefit from the extra structure on "bad days" or in specific situations. As a student's behavior changes, the need for visual supports may change.

Think of visual strategies for supporting communication as *life skills*. It is important to remember *why* students benefit from visually supported communication. We use visual supports because of the student's specific learning style. Their learning style is a part of them. As children grow and mature, their needs may change somewhat, however, it is likely that they will always benefit from visual information and support. Over time, the appearance or content of visual supports may change, but the *value* will remain.

Part 7

CONCLUSION

17
Chapter

Raising And Teaching Successful Students

How to solve the behavior problems of students with autism and other students with communication disorders is a highly controversial topic. The various techniques and approaches currently in use provide a range of results. This book does not answer all the questions and it will not totally close the debates. What it *does* do is provide an important piece to solving the puzzle.

The medical field is continuing to uncover information that will lead to identifying causes and targeting possible medical treatments that have the potential of altering student behavior. Although there continue to be discoveries in biological and neurological research, specialized education remains a significant factor in producing positive long-term changes in student behavior. Unfortunately, even educational approaches can fall short.

The *behavior-communication-visual strategies link* is critically important. "Behavior management" or "compliance training" are frequently the result of a mindset that the student is "being bad" and needs to be brought to a point of obedience. That mindset can lead to discipline that does not create long-term solutions to the student's problems.

It is critically important to recognize that behavior difficulties are frequently directly related to communication breakdowns. Discovering the *causes* of these behaviors reveals that students frequently have difficulty in understanding or problems expressing themselves. As we continue to learn more about *how* these students learn, it becomes obvious that communication is a major link in the behavior mystery. The more we discover how students understand, the better communication partners we can become. The more skillfully students learn to communicate with others, the more appropriately and effectively they will participate in their life activities. Visual strategies support both goals.

Success comes from teaching. An attitude of *"controlling the student's behavior"* (rather than discovering the causes) results in continually reacting to whatever happens. While we attempt to control behaviors, the student may abandon one inappropriate behavior by replacing it with two more. Life can feel like one of those arcade games where you use a hammer to hit the emerging heads. When you hit one of them, two more pop out. By contrast, an attitude of *teaching through improving communication* produces endless opportunities. Much has been written about the intensity of intervention needed for this population. Intensity comes from *capturing the moment*...teaching exactly what skill the student needs to learn in the midst of his or her real life circumstances. Every interaction and every need produces an opportunity for more teaching. Looking at behavior incidents as *opportunities to teach* creates a totally different attitude.

Think of *visual* as the primary form of language for most of these students. Once we identify their strength, the implications are significant. It is imperative that our educational efforts accommodate for how they learn and understand. As communication partners we need to communicate in *their language*.

Behavior problems *will* exist. It is impossible to fix students so they never experience difficulties. That is a natural part of human development.....growing, learning, making mistakes and experiencing conflict. But the frequency and intensity of difficulties can be reduced when the communication environment is supportive.

The goal to aim for is active participation in life routines. The objective is to avoid the behavior challenges that prevent a student from successfully joining family and school activities. The long-term desire is to help students achieve a level of independence in life and to develop some satisfying relationships. Successful outcomes *can* be achieved. *Students do improve as they develop better communication skills. Visual strategies provide a valuable system of communication supports to help make that happen.*

APPENDIX

Footnotes

1. Yarnall, 1997.

2. Frost, 1996

3. Gray, 1994.

References and Additional Reading

Attwood, T. (1998). *Asperger's syndrome: A guide for parents and professionals.* London: Jessica Kingsley Publishers.

Bondy, A. & Frost, L. (1994). The picture exchange communication system. *Focus on Autistic Behavior.* 9 (3), 1-19.

Carr, E. (1985). Behavioral approaches to communication in autism. In E. Schopler & G Mesibov (Eds.), *Communication problems in autism.* New York: Plenum Press.

Cohen, D. & Volkmar, F. (Eds.) (1997). *Handbook of autism and pervasive developmental disorders.* New York: John Wiley and Sons.

Courchene, E. (1991). A new model of brain and behavior development in infantile autism. *Autism Society of America Conference Proceedings.* Indianapolis, IN: ASA.

Dalrymple, N. (1992). *Helpful responses to some of the behaviors of individuals with autism.* Bloomington, IN: Indiana Resource Center for Autism.

Frost, L. and Bondy, A. (1996). *The Picture Exchange Communication System.* Pyramid Educational Consultants.

Fouse, E. & Wheeler, M. (1997). *A treasure chest of behavioral strategies for individuals with autism.* Arlington, TX: Future Horizons.

Gajewski, N., et.al. (1993). *Social star -general interaction skills.* Eau Claire, WI: Thinking Publications.

Goldstein, A. & McGinnis, E. (1997). *Skillstreaming the adolescent.* Champaign, IL: Research Press.

Grandin, T. (1990). *Needs of high functioning teenagers and adults with autism. Focus on Autistic Behavior,* 5(1), 1-16.

Grandin, T. (1991). Autistic perceptions of the world. *Autism Society of America Conference Proceedings.* Indianapolis, IN: ASA.

Grandin, T. (1995). *Thinking in pictures and other reports from my life with autism.* New York: Doubleday.

Gray, C. (1994) *Comic strip conversations.* Arlington, TX: Future Horizons.

Gray, C. (1994). *The new social stories.* Arlington, TX: Future Horizons.

Gray, C. (1993). *Taming the recess jungle.* Arlington, TX: Future Horizons.

Gray, C.A. and Garand, J. D. (1993). Social stories: Improving responses of students with autism with accurate social information. *Focus on Autistic Behavior,* 8(1), 1-10.

Grofer, L. (1990). Helping the child with autism to understand transitions. *The Advocate,* 21(4).

Hodgdon, L. (1991). Solving behavior problems through better communication strategies. *Autism Society of America Conference Proceedings .* Indianapolis, IN: ASA.

Hodgdon, L. (1995). Solving social - behavioral problems through the use of visually supported communication. In K. Quill (Ed.), *Teaching children with autism.* Albany: Delmar Publishing Co.

Hodgdon, L. (1999). *Ten tried and true tools to turn trials into teamwork: Visual tools to enlist cooperation.* Troy: QuirkRoberts Publishing.

Hodgdon, L. (1996). Three favorite techniques to improve communication and avoid frustrations. *The Morning News,* 2, 9-10.

Hodgdon, L. A. (1995) *Visual strategies for improving communication Vol. 1: Practical supports for school and home.* Troy: QuirkRoberts Publishing.

Hodgdon, L. A. (1998). Ten keys to becoming a better communicator. *The Morning News.* 10(3), 8-11.

Hodgdon, L. (1997). *Visual strategies for improving communication. Advocate,* 29(5) 18-19.

La Vigna, G. (1997). Communication training in mute autistic adolescents using the written word. *Journal of Autism and Childhood Schizophrenia,* 7, 135-149.

La Vigna, G. & Donnellan, A. (1986). *Alternatives to punishment: Solving behavior problems with non-aversive strategies.* New York: Irvington.

Mack, A., & Warr-Leeper. (1992). Language abilities in boys with chronic behavior disorders. *Language, speech, and Hearing Services in Schools.* 23, 214-223.

McClannahan, L. & Krantz, P. (1999). *Activity schedules for children with autism teaching independent behavior.* Princeton, NJ: Woodbine House.

McGinnis, E. & Goldstein, A. (1990). *Skillstreaming in early childhood.* Research Press.

McGinnis, E. & Goldstein, A. (1997). *Skillstreaming the elementary school child.* Research Press.

Mehrabian, A. (1972). *Nonverbal communication.* Chicago: Adline Publishing Co.

Mirenda, P., & Santogrossi, J. (1995). A prompt-free strategy to teach pictorial communication system use. *Augmentative and Alternative Communication.* 1, 143-150.

Mirenda, P. & Schuler, A. (1988). Augmenting communication for persons with autism: Issues and strategies. *Topics in Language Disorders.* 9(1), 24-43.

Orelove, F. P. (1982). Developing daily schedules for classrooms of severely handicapped students. *Education and Treatment of Children,* 5, 59-68.

Pierce, K., & Schreibman, L. (1994). Teaching daily living skills to children with autism in unsupervised settings through pictorial self-management. *Journal of Applied Behavior Analysis,* 27, 471-481.

Prizant, B. (1983). Language and communication in autism: Toward an understanding of the "whole" of it. *Journal of Speech and Hearing Disorders.* 48, 296-307.

Prizant, B. & Schuler, A. (1987). Facilitating communication: Theoretical foundations. In Cohen, D. & Donnellan, A. (Eds.) *Handbook of Autism and Pervasive Developmental Disorders.* New York: John Wiley and Sons.

Prizant, B, et.al. (1997). Enhancing language and communication development: Language approaches. In D. Cohen and F. Volkmar (Eds.) *Handbook of Autism and Pervasive Developmental Disorders.* 2nd Edition. New York: John Wiley and Sons.

Quill, K. (Ed.) (1995). *Teaching children with autism: Strategies to enhance communication and socialization.* Albany, NY: Delmar Publishing Co.

Rotholz, D., & Berkowitz, S. (1989). Functionality of two modes of communication in the community by students with developmental disabilities: A comparison of signing and communication books. *Journal of the Association for Persons with Severe Handicaps,* 14, 227-233.

Skjeldal, O., et.al. (1998). Childhood autism: the need for physical investigations. *Brain & Development* 20, 227-233.

Ulliana, L., & Mitchell, R. (1996). *Functional assessment comprehension skills.* New South Wales, Australia: The Autistic Association of New South Wales.

Vaughn, B. & Horner, R. (1995). Effects of concrete versus verbal choice systems on problem behavior. *AAC Augmentative and Alternative Communication* 11, 89-93.

Yarnall, Polly. (1997). Behavior intervention: What's missing? *Autism Society of America Conference Proceedings Insert,.* Milwaukee, WI: ASA.

About The Author

Linda Hodgdon, M.Ed., CCC-SLP is a Speech Pathologist who has specialized in meeting the communication needs of students with autism, other severe communication disorders, and severe behavior disorders. She is a popular national and international presenter who shares her expertise through frequent consultation, conferences and inservice training programs. Linda is well known for her practical, easy to understand, hands-on information.

Solving Behavior Problems In Autism

Improving Communication with Visual Strategies
Linda Hodgdon M.Ed., CCC-SLP

Are you frustrated by the inevitable communication breakdowns and behavior difficulties that occur regularly with your most challenging students???

Then this is the book for you!

• Get lots of Samples & Examples of strategies that have worked to improve communication and solve behavior problems...

• Packed with strategies guaranteed to improve your communication with students who experience autism spectrum disorders or those with moderate to severe communication disorders...

Have you attended one of Linda Hodgdon's Visual Strategies Workshops?

For more information about workshops scheduled or training opportunities, visit

www.LindaHodgdon.com

Find information about workshops, books and visual support materials. Print FREE pictures, read articles and more...

Visit Our Website

www. usevisualstrategies .com

Visual Strategies for Improving Communication

Practical Supports for School and Home

Linda Hodgdon M.Ed., CCC-SLP

This valuable book is **packed**

with strategies guaranteed to improve your communication with students who experience autism... or those with moderate to severe communication disorders...

■ Acquire skills to support communication visually in ways that will significantly improve student performance and reduce or eliminate behavior problems

■ Get lots of practical ideas to support communication in home, school and community settings

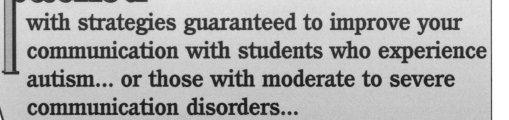
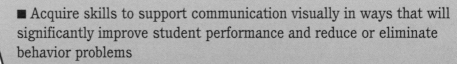

Un libro excelente para patólogos del habla y el lenguaje, educadores, padres y demás personas que trabajan con estudiantes que confrontan dificultades en el área de la comunicación.

Este valioso libro está lleno de estrategias para mejorar la comunicación de los estudiantes que padecen condiciones relacionadas con Autismo, Síndrome de Asperger u otros desafíos de la comunicación.

Obtenga cantidades de ideas para respaldar la comunicación en el hogar y en la escuela.

Linda Hodgdon's dynamic Visual Strategies Workshop is now available in a VIDEO program...

Visual Strategies Workshop Video Program

The **Visual Strategies Workshop** is a 5-video set filmed at a live presentation of Linda Hodgdon's popular and innovative workshop. It provides lots of information about how to use visual strategies and it is packed with samples and examples of visual strategies that have proven successful with students who experience Autism Spectrum Disorders and other moderate to severe communication or behavior challenges. This information is pertinent for every educator or parent who provides support for these students.

VHS or DVD $249.95

*The **Visual Strategies Workshop** is a truly indispensable resource... It is a "must have" for any person, program or organization that provides services to persons with Autism Spectrum Disorders.*
Kathleen S. Pistono, Ph.D.
Consultant in Autism Spectrum Disorders

VIEW
Video Clips on our Website!

Excellent! The programs will be of great benefit to parents, teachers and speech pathologists. . . I know (visual strategies) work!
Tony Attwood, Ph.D.
Author of Asperger's Syndrome

*The **Visual Strategies Workshop** is a wonderful resource that is a timeless, valuable addition to any autism library.*
Carol Gray
Director, The Gray Center
Creator of Social Stories™

*If one picture is worth a thousand words, then the **Visual Strategies Workshop - Video Program** is worth a million! It deserves a treasured place in ones arsenal of educational resources.*
Diane Twachtman-Cullen, Ph.D., CCC-SLP
Executive Director, ADDCON Center

Another View
with Linda Hodgdon

Effective Solutions for Autism, Asperger"s Syndrome and More. . .

June 2005
Volume I, Issue 6

Welcome. . .

What"s in your wallet?

Do you have a photo in your wallet or purse? Your children? Grandchildren? Buster, the family dog? Do you proudly pull that picture out to show your friends or coworkers?

Does producing your prized picture guarantee some questions and conversation. . . ."How old?. . .What"s the name?. . .awww. . How cute. . ." etc. etc. It"s fun to share.

When we search for ways to use visual strategies to improve communication, special photos are an important choice. Photos are great tools to enhance conversation and create deeper relationships. They can be used for multiple purposes.

Today"s article explores how we can use photos to help students build relationships.

Discover the opportunities. . .
With warm regards,

Linda

The **Visual Strategies Workshop - Video Program** is an excellent tool for educators and parents to learn more about using visual strategies to improve communication. The Autism Society of America has chosen **The Visual Strategies Workshop** for its 2004 Excellence in Media Video Award. This program was created for you from information presented in the Visual Strategies Workshops.

For more information . . .

Sign up for Linda Hodgdon's **FREE E-newsletter**, filled with information, teaching ideas, resources and helpfull tips. You'll also get notices of upcoming workshops and new products.

Visit:
www.UseVisualStrategies.com

Order Form

QuirkRoberts Publishing
P. O. Box 71
Troy, MI 48099-0071

Telephone: (248) 879-2598
FAX: (248) 879-2599   Email: info@UseVisualStrategies.com

Order Online:

www.UseVisualStrategies.com

Ship to:

Name _____

Address _____

City _____ State _____ Zip _____

Telephone: Day_____ Evening_____

Payment Options:

❑ Check Enclosed: *Payable to QuirkRoberts Publishing*

❑ Purchase order enclosed P.O.#_____(net 30 days)

❑ Charge to ❑ VISA ❑ MasterCard

Card# _____

Expiration Date: Month_____Year _____

Signature _____

Shipping Charges

U.S.
1 Book $6
2 Books $8

Canada
1 Book $8
2 Books $12

International Orders
$12 per book

VHS or DVD Orders
$20 per program

Shipping charges for larger orders will be determined by weight and destination. Please call if you need exact shipping information.

Please send me:

Quantity	Item	Price Each	TOTAL
	Visual Strategies For Improving Communication	**$39.95**	
	Solving Behavior Problems In Autism	**$39.95**	
	Estrategias Visuales para Mejorar la Comunicación (Spanish)	**$39.95**	
	Visual Strategies Workshop - VHS	**$249.95**	
	Visual Strategies Workshop - DVD	**$249.95**	

Michigan residents add (6%) sales tax....................................
$2.40 per book, $13.00 per VHS / DVD

◄————————————————————— *SHIPPING*

Total

(Payment in U.S. Funds Only)